Asylum and the European Convention on Human Rights

Nuala Mole

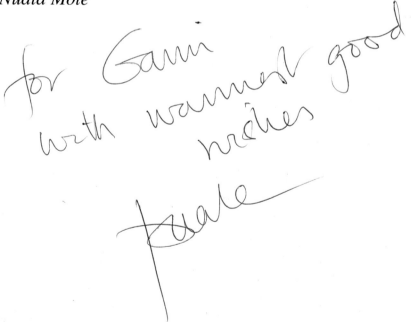

Council of Europe Publishing

French edition:

Le droit d'asile et la Convention européenne des Droits de l'Homme

ISBN 978-92-871-6216-8

Cover design: Council of Europe

Layout: Council of Europe

Council of Europe Publishing
http://book.coe.int
F-67075 Strasbourg Cedex

ISBN 978-92-871-6217-5 *Fourth edition*

This book has also been published in the Human Rights Files series, No. 9 (revised). First published under the title *Problems raised by certain aspects of the present situation of refugees from the standpoint of the European Convention on Human Rights,* Richard Plender, 1984. Second edition, Nuala Mole, 1997. Third edition, 2000. Fourth edition, 2007.

*N*uala Mole is Director of the AIRE Centre (Advice on Individual Rights in Europe), a voluntary organisation in London which provides information and advice on the rights of individuals under international human rights law and the law of the European Union. The centre also provides legal representation before the European Court of Human Rights. As with previous editions the author has been greatly assisted by several members of the AIRE Centre's team – Andrew McCann, David Norris, Nawazish Choudhury, Laura Wrage, Anita Goh, Maryam Tabib, Adam Weiss, Vanessa Schmidt – but most particularly by the tireless efforts of Catherine Meredith. The author is also grateful to Dr Maria Teresa Gil Bazo of Newcastle University, Professor Guy Goodwin Gill of the University of Oxford and Frances Nicholson of UNHCR for their particular assistance and to many other colleagues in Europe and further afield, both practitioners and academics, on whose experience and erudition she has drawn. Any errors nevertheless inevitably remain her own.*

Contents

Introduction

In many parts of Europe (and at least in the 27 of the 47 Council of Europe member states which are now also members of the European Union)[1], there exist four simultaneous and, often, overlapping key legal regimes for the international protection of asylum seekers and refugees. These are:

- the 1951 Geneva Convention relating to the Status of Refugees (the Geneva Convention) and its 1967 Protocol;

- the law of the European Union (EU law);[2]

- the 1984 United Nations Convention against Torture and other Cruel, Inhuman or Degrading Treatment or Punishment (UNCAT); and

- the 1950 Convention for the Protection of Human Rights and Fundamental Freedoms (ECHR) and its protocols.

In addition all member states of the Council of Europe are also parties to the various other UN human rights treaties, in particular the 1966 International Covenant on Civil and Political Rights (ICCPR), which offers broadly comparable protection to that of the ECHR. For reasons of space, reference is only made in this book to the most important case law of the UN Human Rights Committee, as the supervisory body for the ICCPR. Other UN key human rights instruments (for example, the 1948 Universal Declaration of Human Rights (UDHR), the 1979 Convention on the Elimination of All Forms of Discrimination against Women (CEDAW), the 1965 Convention on the Elimination of All Forms of Racial Discrimination (CERD) and the 1989 Convention on the Rights of the Child (CRC)) may also be relevant to asylum issues.

This book is about the standards of protection offered by the ECHR. However, the standards of some or all of the other legal regimes are, in many cases, part and parcel of those standards and are referred to as and when appropriate.

---

1 Not all EU states are bound by all measures: see the section on EU measures below.

2 EU member states are required to transpose directives in time and to implement them fully. If they fail to do so they must pay compensation to individuals who suffer as a result of their failure to do so. See *Francovich and Bonifaci v. Italy* (Cases C-6 and 9/90 [1991] ECR I-5357).

There are many individuals whose situation falls outside the scope of the Geneva Convention, of the UNCAT and of the EU measures, but who are protected by the European Convention on Human Rights. In the following pages the standards of the Geneva Convention, the UNCAT, and the applicable EU regulations and directives will all be referred to when considering the standards of the ECHR.

This may be because the Convention prohibits its arbitrariness and so requires that decisions are in accordance with the law – which for EU states includes EU law – or it may be simply because Article 53 of the ECHR provides "Nothing in this Convention shall be construed as limiting or derogating from any of the human rights and fundamental freedoms which may be ensured under the laws of any High Contracting Party or under any other agreement to which it is a Party". The European Court has, however, frequently stated that it has no power to rule on whether a state has acted in conformity with its obligations under other treaties except insofar as it is required to determine whether an interference with rights guaranteed.

The Geneva Convention relating to the Status of Refugees is the *lex specialis* of asylum in Europe and its pre-eminence as the key international instrument for protecting those who fall within its scope is unquestioned. It provides those people with an ample basket of rights and privileges. This short guide makes frequent references to the protection offered by the Geneva Convention, but for reasons of space and because this text is primarily about the ECHR, those references are brief and thus perforce incomplete.

In addition, many of those now seeking international protection in Europe do not fall within the mandate of the Geneva Convention or have problems and needs which the convention does not address. This book examines the parallel protection offered by the ECHR.

The Council of Europe Convention for the Prevention of Torture (1987) set up a system for monitoring all places where people are deprived of their liberty. The European Committee for the Prevention of Torture (CPT) makes periodic visits to all contracting states and publishes (with the consent of the state) reports on the visits. It also produces General Reports. Although the CPT itself cannot make legal findings that states have violated the prohibition on torture or inhuman and degrading treatment – only the Court can do that – it can make factual findings. Its reports carry great weight and are often relied on by the Court when examining complaints. Both the country reports and the General Reports have frequently looked at both the legal and physical conditions in which asylum seekers and other immigration detainees have been held. The work of the committee is referred to throughout this book.

The pages that follow are divided into three sections.

Part One of this handbook looks at the approach taken to date by the ECtHR to the extraterritorial application of those articles in connection with the risks faced on expulsion to the proposed country of destination. The section explores the possible future extraterritorial application of those articles on which no ruling had as yet been made.

Part Two examines the application of the articles to asylum issues other than the extraterritorial application of the Convention's provisions.

Part Three concerns the subsidiary protection of the Convention organs.

Overview

A key attribute of national sovereignty is the right of states to admit or exclude aliens from their territory.[3] Only if exclusion from the territory or from protection would involve a breach of some other provision of international law are states bound to admit aliens. The concept of asylum is the most important example of the latter principle. Although Article 14 of the UDHR expressly protects the right to "seek and enjoy asylum from persecution", this right is not found in the texts of other general instruments of international human rights law such as the ICCPR or the European Convention on Human Rights. When those human rights instruments were drafted it was thought that the 1951 Geneva Convention relating to the Status of Refugees would constitute a *lex specialis* which fully covered the need, and no express provision on asylum was thus included.

The Geneva Convention treats those who are recognised as falling within the scope of its protection as a privileged group and provides them with a comprehensive bundle of rights. In the early years of the Geneva Convention recognition as a refugee in Europe was not a problem. Everyone knew who refugees were. UNHCR saw no need to produce a handbook to guide asylum determination procedures until 1979. In the new millennium, European governments tend to apply the Geneva Convention's provisions in an increasingly legalistic way and thereby contain their responsibilities towards people at risk of ill-treatment who might otherwise be able to find the protection from expulsion which the Geneva Convention was designed, in part, to provide. That role is now arguably more effectively performed in the European context by general human rights instruments and in particular by the European Convention on Human Rights.

The Geneva Convention remains effective – and essential – as an instrument which provides additional benefits to an increasingly smaller number of people who are recognised as falling within its ambit by governments. However, many of those who need international protection because they are at risk of expulsion to situations where they would face serious harm such as torture or inhuman and degrading treatment or punishment, or whose expulsion

---

3 See, amongst many others, *Salah Sheekh v. the Netherlands*, Application No. 1948/04, judgment of 11 January 2007, paragraph 135.

would in itself constitute such treatment, fall outside the ambit of the Geneva Convention, for instance because no nexus or link can be established between the persecution feared and one of the five convention grounds.[4]

The new EU regime fills some of these lacunae but still fails to apply to all those who are recognised by the European Court of Human Rights as being in need of and entitled to international protection. Even if not actually expelled, those who are refused recognition as refugees and not otherwise granted the appropriate subsidiary (or complementary) protection are often left drifting in a state of undocumented uncertainty.

Both the European Convention on Human Rights, which was opened for signature in November 1950, and the Geneva Convention, which was opened for signature the following year, were drafted as the polarisation in international relations which marked the Cold War set in. Both conventions reflect the concerns and thinking of the period. Over the next fifty years, when the conflict between the two opposing ideologies dominated international relations, the definition of a refugee set out in Article 1A, paragraph 2,[5] and the principle of *non-refoulement* established in Article 33, paragraph 1,[6] of the Geneva Convention became well recognised in international law. Drafted in the wake of the massive forced displacement at the time of the Second World War, the Geneva Convention was designed to provide a legal status for those persons who found themselves outside their country of nationality or habitual residence and in fear of persecution as a consequence of "events occurring in Europe before 1 January 1951".

The European Convention on Human Rights, on the other hand, was intended to provide a legal regional recognition of most of the rights set out in the Universal Declaration of Human Rights (UDHR) and to provide international mechanisms to police their implementation. It did not, however, contain any express provision to reflect Article 14 of the UDHR, which guarantees the right to seek and enjoy asylum from persecution.

---

4 Under the Geneva Convention a well-founded fear of persecution must be "for reasons of" race, religion, nationality, membership of a particular social group or political opinion.

5 Article 1A, paragraph 2, defines a refugee as someone who "owing to well-founded fear of being persecuted for reasons of race, religion, nationality, membership of a particular social group or political opinion, is outside the country of his nationality and is unable or, owing to such a fear, unwilling to avail himself of the protection of that country; or who, not having a nationality and being outside the country of his former habitual residence as a result of such events, is unable or, owing to such fear, is unwilling to return to it ...".

6 Article 33, paragraph 1, states: "No Contracting State shall expel or return ('refouler') a refugee in any manner whatsoever to the frontiers of territories where his life or freedom would be threatened on account of his race, religion, nationality, membership of a particular social group or political opinion."

Background considerations: movement of refugees in Europe from the aftermath of the Second World War to the present

There is a long history of people seeking international protection in Europe. While the Geneva Convention was primarily an instrument devised to meet a humanitarian need by providing a proper legal framework for asylum, it was also an instrument which was intended to serve the aims of Cold War politics. The emphasis was on providing protection for those who fled from those countries behind the Iron Curtain where the furtherance of collective communist ideals took precedence over the observance of the civil and political rights of the individual. The declared sympathies of such refugees were with Western political values.

In 1967 the New York Protocol to the Geneva Convention removed the reference to 1 January 1951,[7] and almost all the countries[8] which were then members of the Council of Europe subsequently removed the geographical limitation so that those who arrived from any part of the world were protected. This was recognition that the refugee question was not simply an isolated European phenomenon. During the years of rapid economic expansion of the 1960s, the Cold War meant that very few refugees or asylum seekers were able to reach Western countries and arrivals were, in any case, welcomed to feed the expanding economies' demand for increased labour.

The first oil crisis in 1973 and the resulting recession brought growing unemployment and opposition to new immigration. Less than thirty years after the fall of the Nazi regime in Germany, the ugly spectre of racism was also beginning to haunt Europe again.

At the same time, events such as Idi Amin's seizure of power in Uganda in 1971 and General Pinochet's coup in Chile in 1973 prompted thousands to flee the repression which followed in those countries. Although the overwhelming majority of refugees from any conflict or oppression still tend to flee only as far as neighbouring countries, the increasing availability of air travel meant that some were able to reach the developed world. The numbers involved were, however, small compared with the large numbers of both refugees and migrants it was feared might arrive after the fall of the Iron Curtain in November 1989 and the crumbling of the eastern bloc, where movement had previously been tightly controlled.

States have found their commitment to their obligations under international law strained as a result of this greater freedom of movement, while legitimate

---

7 New York Protocol to the Geneva Convention, 1967, Article 1, paragraph 2.

8 Of the present Council of Europe member states, only Monaco and Turkey still retain it. For information see: www.unhcr.org/protect/PROTECTION/3b73b)d63.pdf.

concerns have also arisen that economic migrants may be misusing asylum legislation in an attempt to secure entry to countries which have closed normal immigration routes.[9]

Recent trends in Europe

The vast majority of asylum seekers arriving in Europe since the end of the Cold War have fled countries where serious human rights abuses are endemic – countries racked by civil war or countries where the machinery of the state has broken down to such a degree that it can no longer offer protection to its citizens. The early 1990s saw a significant increase in the number of asylum applications in Europe, largely as a result of the Balkan wars and an exodus of people from the countries of the former Yugoslavia. The late 1990s brought about yet another rise in applications during the Kosovo crisis, in particular the events of the spring of 1999, which brought about refugee movements in Europe on a scale unseen since the Second World War.

While many of those seeking protection came from within the Council of Europe itself (for example, Turkish Kurds or Roma from the former communist states), others were fleeing repression and civil war in countries further afield such as Sri Lanka, Somalia, the Democratic Republic of the Congo (DRC), Rwanda and Algeria. The trend in the first few years of the new millennium has shown an increase in asylum seekers from Afghanistan and Iraq. Indeed, nationals of Iraq and Afghanistan, along with those from China, the former Federal Republic of Yugoslavia, the Russian Federation (mainly Chechens) and Turkey, currently account for the majority of asylum applications in the world's industrialised nations.

While Europe continues to register significant numbers of asylum applications, general trends are, however, showing a major decrease in the number of people applying for asylum in recent years, to the level of the early 1980s.

The expansion of the European Union on 1 May 2004 from 15 to 25 member states and to 27 on 1 January 2007 also extended the EU's external borders. Some of these new member states, such as Slovakia and Poland, but particularly Malta, have experienced a significant increase in asylum applications.

The member states of the EU have sought to develop a comprehensive common European asylum policy, the latest phase of which is contained in the "Hague Programme", which is, at the time of writing, almost complete.

A section of this book deals with the measures adopted at EU level insofar as they are relevant to the application of the ECHR. A list of all the relevant EU measures – which now normally regulate asylum in most of the member states of the EU and thus more than half the member states of the Council of Europe – is appended.

---

9 See Nicholson, F. and Twomey, P. (eds.), *Refugee rights and realities*, Cambridge University Press, 1999.

Most of those in need of international protection find themselves seeking asylum in member states of the Council of Europe which are outside the EU. Many would prefer to be able to travel on to the EU states where there are established communities of the groups to which they belong and where support networks and thus work opportunities exist. Refugees failing to reach Western European countries remain in the member states of the Council of Europe in central and eastern Europe and the former Soviet Union and in some cases in the Mediterranean. These states are under considerable strain as they often lack the mechanisms, legislation, experience, or appropriate resources to handle their caseload.

The provisions of the European Convention on Human Rights now bind 47 countries (as at 9 October 2007).[10] The experience of the Council of Europe in brokering agreements, conventions, recommendations, resolutions and declarations complementary to refugee instruments, the forum for discussion which it offers and the body of case law built up by the European Commission and Court of Human Rights is invaluable in assisting these states – indeed, all Council of Europe member states – to ensure that their humanitarian obligations under international law are upheld and the rights of refugees protected.[11] The Council of Europe unit which was previously dedicated to refugee issues (CAHAR) has now been disbanded.

---

10 The date at which Monaco became a party. Serbia and Montenegro acceded on 3 April 2003 and have now separated. The accession of the independent Montenegro took place on 11 May 2007.

11 A list of Council of Europe instruments relating to refugees is attached in Appendix I at page 137.

Part One – The role of the European Convention on Human Rights in protection from expulsion to face human rights abuses

Whilst UNHCR keeps a vigilant watch on the way in which national authorities comply with their obligations, the Geneva Convention has no formal international supervision procedure to review the correctness of individual decisions to recognise, or withhold recognition of, refugee status. There is no right of individual petition to a judicial body comparable to that which exists under Articles 34[12] and 35[13] of the European Convention on Human Rights. A large body of specialised case law has developed on its interpretation and application by national courts. But there is no uniformity of approach and the result has been a patchwork of disparate decisions. This lack of consistency in approach to the determination of refugee status was one of the problems identified by the EU and addressed in the "Qualification Directive" (EU Directive 2004/83), which had to be transposed into the law of all EU member states by October 2006. The definitions contained in the directive, even of the meaning to be given to the provisions of the Geneva Convention, are EU definitions and do not necessarily reflect the views of UNHCR.

The directive states in its preamble (4) that the Common European Asylum System "should include, in the short term, the approximation of rules on the recognition of refugees and the content of refugee status". In its preamble (6) it states that its main objective is "on the one hand, to ensure that member states apply common criteria for the identification of persons genuinely in need of international protection, and, on the other hand, to ensure that a

---

12 Article 34 states: "The Court may receive Application from any person, non-governmental organisation or group of individuals claiming to be the victim of a violation by one of the High Contracting Parties of the rights set forth in the Convention or the protocols thereto. The High Contracting Parties undertake not to hinder in any way the effective exercise of this right."

13 Article 35, paragraph 1, states: "The Court may only deal with the matter after all domestic remedies have been exhausted, according to the generally recognised rules of international law, and within a period of six months from the date on which the final decision was taken."

minimum level of benefits is available for these persons in all member states". In defining "acts of persecution" in connection with the recognition of Geneva Convention refugee status for the purposes of the directive, the directive provides in Article 9, paragraph 1(a), that such acts must be sufficiently serious by their nature or repetition as to constitute a severe violation of basic human rights, in particular the rights from which no derogation is permitted under Article 15, paragraph 2, of the ECHR.[14] The directive makes no reference, however, to the ECHR when defining "serious harm" the risk of which entitles people to "subsidiary protection".[15]

1. The applicability of the Convention to asylum cases

Although the Qualification Directive makes passing reference to the ECHR, there is no express provision relating to asylum contained in the European Convention on Human Rights and it might therefore seem to be of only marginal relevance to those seeking asylum in Europe.[16] This is far from the case. The substantial body of jurisprudence that has emerged from the Convention organs between 1989 and 2007 now sets the standards for the rights of asylum seekers across Europe.

The first issue considered by the Convention organs and eventually ruled on by the Court was whether the European Convention on Human Rights applied at all to asylum situations. The Court has repeatedly stated that there is no right to asylum as such in the Convention or its protocols.[17] Whilst the Geneva Convention protected those at risk of persecution, it was Article 3 of the UN Convention against Torture which was the first provision of an international human rights treaty which expressly prohibited expulsion to face the risk of torture.

---

14 "No derogation from Article 2 except in respect of deaths arising from lawful acts of war, or from Articles 3, 4(1), and 7 shall be made under this provision."

15 The other key EU provision refers only to those seeking recognition as Geneva Convention refugees.

16 A number of other international instruments also affect the rights of asylum seekers: the Universal Declaration of Human Rights, Articles 13 and 14; the International Covenant on Civil and Political Rights, Articles 12 and 13; the International Convention on the Elimination of All Forms of Racial Discrimination, Articles 5.d.i and ii; the United Nations Convention against Torture and Other Cruel, Inhuman or Degrading Treatment or Punishment, Article 3; the Convention on the Status of Stateless Persons, Articles 27 and 28; the Organization of African Unity's Refugee Convention (1969); the Organization of American States' Declaration; the United Nations Declaration on Territorial Asylum; and the United Nations Declaration on the Human Rights of Individuals who are not Nationals of the Country where they Live.

17 *Vilvarajah and Others v. the United Kingdom*, Application Nos. 13163/87, 13164/87 and 13165/87, judgment of 30 October 1991, paragraph 102, *Salah Sheek v. the Netherlands*, Application No. 1948/04, judgment of 13 January 2007.

However, the European Court ruled that it would not be compatible with the "common heritage of political traditions, ideals, freedom and rule of law" to which the Preamble refers, were a Contracting State to the ECHR knowingly to surrender a person to another state where there were substantial grounds for believing that he or she would be in danger of being subjected to torture or inhuman or degrading treatment or punishment.[18]

From the 1960s the Commission and the Court have regularly considered the question of whether extradition, expulsion, or deportation to a country where an individual is likely to be subjected to such treatment is contrary to Article 3.[19] The question of applicability was first considered in detail by the European Court of Human Rights in the case of *Soering v. the United Kingdom*, a case concerning not political asylum but extradition.[20] The US State of Virginia wished to extradite Mr Soering from Britain to stand trial on capital charges. At the time prisoners in Virginia often remained on death row awaiting execution for between six and eight years. It was alleged that this constituted inhuman and degrading treatment contrary to Article 3.

The Court noted the existence of other international instruments, such as the Geneva Convention and the UN Convention against Torture, which expressly and specifically address the question of sending individuals to a country where they will be exposed to the risk of prohibited treatment. It nevertheless found that the application of the European Convention on Human Rights was not excluded by the existence of the other instruments. Their existence could not "absolve the Contracting Parties from responsibility under Article 3 for all and any foreseeable consequences of extradition suffered outside their jurisdiction".[21]

The Court observed:

> "The fact that a specialised treaty should spell out in detail a specific obligation attaching to a prohibition on torture does not mean that an essentially similar obligation is not already inherent in the general terms of Article 3."[22]

The Court noted that the object and purpose of the Convention as an instrument for the protection of individual human beings require that its provisions

---

18 *Soering v. the United Kingdom*, Application No. 14038/88, judgment of 7 July 1989, paragraph 88.

19 See, for example, *Soering v. the United Kingdom*, Application No. 14038/88, judgment of 7 July 1989; *Cruz Varas v. Sweden*, Application No. 15576/89, judgment of 20 March 1991; *Vilvarajah and Others v. the United Kingdom*, Application Nos. 13163/87, 13164/87 and 13165/87, judgment of 30 October 1991; *Nasri v. France*, Application No. 19465/92, judgment of 13 July 1995.

20 *Soering v. the United Kingdom*, Application No. 14038/88, judgment of 7 July 1989.

21 Ibid., p. 26, paragraph 86.

22 Ibid., p. 26, paragraph 88.

be interpreted and applied so as to make its safeguards practical and effective.[23] It found that the inherent obligation under Article 3 also extends to cases in which the fugitive would be faced in the receiving state by a real risk of exposure to inhuman or degrading treatment proscribed by that article. The Court noted that:

> "It is a liability incurred by the Contracting State by reason of its having taken action which has as a direct consequence the exposure of an individual to such treatment."[24]

Shortly after the judgment in *Soering*, the case of *Cruz Varas v. Sweden* came before the Court. It was the first case which concerned a refused asylum seeker. The Court held that the principle enunciated in *Soering* applied to decisions to expel as well as to extradite.[25] This view was reaffirmed in the judgment in *Vilvarajah v. the United Kingdom*.[26]

The question of the applicability of Article 3 to expulsion cases is now generally considered to be established beyond doubt. As late as 1995, the United Kingdom Government nevertheless still tried to put forward the contrary argument in the case of *Chahal*.[27] This was firmly rejected by the Commission, which reaffirmed the principle laid down in *Vilvarajah*:

> "Expulsion by the Contracting State of an asylum seeker may give rise to an issue under Article 3, and hence engage the responsibility of that State under the Convention, where substantial grounds have been shown for believing that the person concerned faced a real risk of being subjected to torture or to inhuman or degrading treatment or punishment in the country to which he was returned."[28]

The government eventually accepted the applicability of the Convention in its pleadings before the Court.[29]

The position was succinctly put recently in the judgment in *Salah Sheekh*:

> "The right to political asylum is not contained in either the Convention or its Protocols. However, in exercising their right to expel such aliens, Contracting States must have regard to Article 3 of the Convention which enshrines one of the fundamental values of democratic societies and prohibits in absolute terms torture or

---

23 Ibid., p. 27, paragraph 90.

24 Ibid., p. 27, paragraph 91.

25 *Cruz Varas v. Sweden*, Application No. 15576/89, judgment of 20 March 1991, paragraph 70.

26 *Vilvarajah and Others v. the United Kingdom*, Application Nos. 13163/87, 13164/87 and 13165/87, judgment of 30 October 1991, p. 32, paragraph 103.

27 *Chahal v. the United Kingdom*, Application No. 22414/93, report of 27 June 1995.

28 *Vilvarajah and Others v. the United Kingdom*, op. cit.

29 *Chahal v. the United Kingdom*, Application No. 22414/93, report of 27 June 1995, paragraph 74.

inhuman or degrading treatment or punishment, irrespective of the victim's conduct, however undesirable or dangerous. The expulsion of an alien may give rise to an issue under this provision, and hence engage the responsibility of the expelling State under the Convention, where substantial grounds have been shown for believing that the person in question, if expelled, would face a real risk of being subjected to treatment contrary to Article 3 in the receiving country. In such circumstances, Article 3 implies an obligation not to expel the individual to that country."[30]

While the Commission and Court have most frequently considered asylum issues in the context of Article 3, it is clear that it is not the only Convention article relevant to asylum questions. As is set out below, the processing of applications for asylum may also raise issues of return to face risks under Article 2 (right to life), Article 4 (prohibition of slavery, servitude, and compulsory labour), Article 5 (right to liberty and security of the person), Article 6 (right to a fair trial), Article 7 (prohibition on retroactive criminal punishment), Article 8 (right to respect for family and private life), Article 9 (right to freedom of thought, conscience, and religion), Article 10 (freedom of expression), Article 11 (freedom of assembly and association), Article 14 (prohibition of discrimination in the enjoyment of Convention rights), Article 16 (restrictions on political activity of aliens), Article 4 of Protocol No. 4 (collective expulsion of aliens), Article 1 of Protocol No. 7 (procedural safeguards relating to expulsion of aliens), Article 3 of Protocol No. 7 (exclusion of own nationals), Article 4 of Protocol No. 7 (prohibition on double jeopardy), Protocol No. 12 (general prohibition on discrimination).

2. The protection from expulsion to face treatment contrary to Article 3 – An absolute right

The Court has repeatedly stressed in cases involving extradition, expulsion or deportation of individuals to third countries that Article 3 prohibits in *absolute* terms expulsion to face torture or inhuman or degrading treatment or punishment and that its guarantees apply irrespective of the authors of the risk, the context of the risk, or the conduct of the applicant.

There are a number of key differences between the protection guaranteed by the ECHR and that of the other legal regimes offering international protection.

Alienage

To attract the protection of the Geneva Convention a person must, under Article 1 of that instrument, be outside the country of his or her nationality or habitual residence. However, the European Convention on Human Rights has a wider application. The Commission considered in the case of *Fadele*

---

30 *Salah Sheek v. the Netherlands*, Application No. 1948/04, judgment of 11 January 2007, paragraph 135.

v. the United Kingdom[31] that Article 3 could apply to cases where British citizen children were being constructively exiled from the United Kingdom by the deportation of their custodial parent and where the conditions which they would face on return could amount to inhuman and degrading treatment.

The same reasoning as was applied in *Fadele* would apply to situations where a refused asylum seeker's close family members include, as they sometimes do, nationals of the expelling state. The constructive deportation of such nationals might infringe Article 3 (taken together with Article 8) if it could be shown they would be exposed to the risk of ill-treatment should they accompany the refused asylum seeker. The same principle would also apply to the extradition of a state's own nationals. Such situations also raise issues under Article 3 of Protocol No. 4 to the Convention, which states that:

> "1. No one shall be expelled, by means either of an individual or of a collective measure, from the territory of the state of which he is a national.

> No one shall be deprived of the right to enter the territory of a state of which he is a national."[32]

The United Kingdom is not a party to Protocol No. 4 so no issues under that provision arose in the *Fadele* case.

Persecution for a "Convention reason"

To attract the protection of the Geneva Convention a person must fear "persecution" for one or more of the reasons set out in Article 1A, paragraph 2, of that instrument: "race, religion, nationality, membership of a particular social group or political opinion".

Under the Geneva Convention, it is not only a well-founded fear of persecution which needs to be present but also the reasons for that fear of persecution.

No similar qualification applies to Article 3 of the European Convention on Human Rights. If there is a real risk of exposure to ill-treatment the reasons for it are immaterial. Article 3 applies equally in cases of extradition. It applies to the removal of refused asylum seekers or of those who have been granted humanitarian status, but are not recognised Geneva Convention refugees, or to those who have been recognised as refugees but have lost the protection of the Geneva Convention.

The case of *H.L.R. v. France*[33] concerned a convicted drug dealer who had provided evidence at his trial which had led to the conviction of several other

---

31 *Fadele v. the United Kingdom,* Application No. 13078/87, decision of 12 February 1990.

32 This provision could not be invoked in the case of *Fadele* as the United Kingdom is not a party to Protocol No. 4. It was noted by Fawcett in the report on the *East African Asians* case that the failure to admit nationals may be a breach of Article 3 (Report, paragraph 242, 3 EHRR 76, 1973).

33 *H.L.R. v. France,* Application No. 24573/94, judgment of 29 April 1997.

members of a Colombian drugs ring and had significantly impeded its operation. On his release from prison he was to be returned to Colombia where he
would have been at risk from revenge by the members of the cartel. The Court
held that, if he was at risk, the reasons for his anticipated ill-treatment were
not material to the protection guaranteed under Article 3.

D. v. the United Kingdom[34] concerned the proposed expulsion of a person dying
of Aids to his home country where he had no family or material resources,
where there was no social welfare provision available to him and no treatment for
Aids. He was in no sense being persecuted for a Geneva Convention reason.
The Court found that his expulsion would constitute a violation of Article 3.

Article 3 of the UNCAT prohibits expulsion, return or extradition to "another
State where there are substantial grounds for believing that he would be in
danger of being subjected to torture". The fact of the risk of torture is what is
important, not the reasons for it.

State responsibility – The source of the risk

State responsibility for the feared persecution was considered an inherent part
of the definition contained in Article 1 of the Geneva Convention, which safeguards the situation of those who have for one reason or another lost the
protection of their own state. Under the Geneva Convention it is generally
considered that a refugee must fear persecution either by the state itself or
because the state is unable or unwilling to provide protection to the person
concerned. In contrast, the Court held in *Soering v. the United Kingdom* that
in looking at the responsibility of the expelling state under Article 3 of the
European Convention on Human Rights: "There is no question of adjudicating
on or establishing the responsibility of the receiving country."[35]

A minority of European states were unwilling to recognise as refugees those
whose claims relate to persecution by "non-state agents", such as terrorist
groups, guerrilla armies, or where there is a civil war; or also family members,
for example in cases of domestic violence (although as indicated below this
has changed for EU states with the adoption of the Qualification Directive).

It was, for instance, argued before the Court[36] that since the United Nations
Convention against Torture expressly provides that ill-treatment must involve
the responsibility of state authorities, the European Convention on Human
Rights should be applied in the same way. In *T.I. v. the United Kingdom*[37] the

---

34 *D. v. the United Kingdom,* Application No. 30240/96, judgment of 2 May 1997.

35 *Soering v. the United Kingdom,* Application No. 14038/88, judgment of 7 July 1989,
    p. 27, paragraph 91.

36 See, for example, *H.L.R. v. France,* Application No. 24573/94, judgment of 29 April 1997.

37 *T.I. v. the United Kingdom,* Application No. 43844/98, decision of 7 March 2000. The
    Court declared it inadmissible.

Court noted that the German courts not only excluded persecution by non-state agents as a ground for asylum, but, despite the jurisprudence of the European Court, in applying the provision of their law which expressly refers to Article 3 of the European Convention on Human Rights, they did recognise threats from non-state agents as qualifying an individual for subsidiary protection under that provision. In *Tatete v. Switzerland*[38] the Swiss Government had also argued that the Convention did not apply because the risk did not emanate from agents of the state.

The Court has expressly rejected this argument in several cases. In *Ahmed v. Austria,*[39] the applicant was threatened with return to Somalia, a country at the time in the grip of various warlords and with no government as such, and consequently no state to exercise responsibility. The Convention organs considered that the absence of state authority was immaterial to the risk to which the applicant would be exposed. The Court reiterated this view in *H.L.R. v. France.*[40] The French Government sought to argue before the Commission and the Court[41] that as other international instruments, such as the United Nations Convention against Torture and Other Inhuman or Degrading Treatment or Punishment, expressly provide that the ill-treatment must involve the responsibility of state authorities, the Convention should be interpreted in this way too. In *D. v. the United Kingdom*[42] it was accepted by all parties that the Government of St Kitts (D.'s country of origin) could not be held responsible for the poverty of the island that led to the absence of the socio-medical support on which the applicant relied in the United Kingdom. The same principle has also been applied in *B.B. v. France.*[43]

In *Ammari v. Sweden*[44] the applicant claimed that he was at risk of being subjected to treatment contrary to Article 3, not only by the Algerian authorities but also by the Armed Islamic Group (GIA). The Court stated that "owing to the absolute character of the right guaranteed, it cannot be ruled out that Article 3 may also apply where the danger emanates from persons or groups of persons who are not public officials". The Court further stated that the risk must be "real" and that the authorities of the receiving state are not able to obviate the risk by providing appropriate protection.

---

38 *Tatete v. Switzerland*, Application No. 41874/98, judgment of 24 June 1998.

39 *Ahmed v. Austria*, Application No. 25964/94, judgment of 17 December 1996.

40 *H.L.R. v. France*, Application No. 24573/94, judgment of 29 April 1997.

41 *H.L.R. v. France*, Government Memorial, Court (96) 322.

42 *D. v. the United Kingdom*, Application No. 30240/96, judgment of 2 May 1997.

43 *B.B. v. France*, Application No. 30930/96, judgment of 7 September 1998.

44 *Ammari v. Sweden*, Application No. 60959/00, decision of 22 October 2002.

The EU Qualification Directive (Article 6) lists the "actors of persecution or serious harm" as:

"(a) the State;

(b) parties or organisations controlling the State or a substantial part of the territory of the State;

(c) non-State actors, if it can be demonstrated that the actors mentioned in (a) and (b), including international organisations, are unable or unwilling to provide protection against persecution or serious harm as defined in Article 7."

Since the adoption of the Qualification Directive, all EU states are therefore required to recognise persecution by non-state agents as falling within the refugee definition.

The approach of the UN Committee against Torture requires the threat to result from state action or acquiescence, or acts by groups exercising quasi-governmental authority (see page 50 below).

The recent judgment of the Court in *Salah Sheekh*[45] makes the position under the ECHR quite clear:

"The existence of the obligation not to expel is not dependent on whether the source of the risk of the treatment stems from factors which involve the responsibility, direct or indirect, of the authorities of the receiving country, and Article 3 may thus also apply in situations where the danger emanates from persons or groups of persons who are not public officials."[46]

Exclusion clauses

Article 1F of the Geneva Convention states that:

"The provisions of this Convention shall not apply to any person with respect to whom there are serious reasons for considering that:

(a) He has committed a crime against peace, a war crime, or a crime against humanity, as defined in the international instruments drawn up to make provision in respect of such crimes;

(b) He has committed a serious non-political crime outside the country of refuge prior to his admission to that country as a refugee;

(c) He has been guilty of acts contrary to the purposes and principles of the United Nations."

This curious exception crept into the Geneva Convention during the *travaux préparatoires*. As a leading commentator has observed:

"It is difficult to see why a person who, before becoming a refugee has been convicted of a serious crime and has served his sentence, should forever be debarred from

---

45 *Salah Sheekh v. the Netherlands*, Application No. 1948/04, judgment of 13 January 2007.

46 Ibid., paragraph 147.

refugee status. Such a rule would seem to run counter to the generally accepted principle of penal law that a person who has been punished for an offence should suffer no further prejudice on account of the offence committed."[47]

In the case of *Paez v. Sweden*[48] the applicant had been excluded from recognition as a refugee and refused asylum in Sweden as his case was found to fall within Article 1F of the Geneva Convention. But when his brother, who had a similar case, won before the UN Committee against Torture on 28 April 1997, the Swedish Government felt constrained to grant both brothers protection from expulsion.

As was noted at the outset, international human rights law provides protection to all human beings and that protection is absolute where Article 3 is engaged. The Geneva Convention provides protection for only a privileged group of people at risk of persecution for a "Convention reason" and that protection can be lost if the exclusion clauses apply.

Article 33, paragraph 1, of the Geneva Convention affirms that no one shall be returned *(refoulé)*:

"in any manner whatsoever to the frontiers of territories where his [or her] life or freedom would be threatened on account of his race, religion, nationality, membership of a particular social group or political opinion."

However, this protection is lost if Article 33, paragraph 2, applies. This states:

"A refugee may lose the protection of the Geneva Convention if there are reasonable grounds for regarding him as a danger to the security of the country in which he is or if he is convicted of a particularly serious crime and constitutes a danger to the community."

The application of Article 33, paragraph 2, is constrained by Article 32, which stipulates a refugee may only be expelled "on grounds of national security or public order" and that such an expulsion may only be "in pursuance of a decision reached in accordance with due process of law". Any determination of whether or not one of the exceptions provided for in Article 33, paragraph 2, is applicable must be made in a procedure which offers adequate safeguards, that is, an individualised determination by the country of asylum that the person concerned constitutes a present or future danger to the security or the community of the host country. Nevertheless, those found to present such a threat can lose their protection from return under the Geneva Convention.

The protection accorded by Article 3 of the European Convention on Human Rights is not limited in this way. This was stated by the Court in *Soering,* a

---

47 Weis P., "The concept of the refugee in international law", *Journal du droit international,* 87, 1960, p. 928 at pp. 984-6, cited in Hathaway, *The law of refugee status,* Butterworths, 1991.

48 *Paez v. Sweden,* Application No. 29482/95, judgment of 30 October 1997.

case concerning extradition to face charges of a brutal murder allegedly committed before admission to the territory of the respondent state. The Court held:

> "It would hardly be compatible with the underlying values of the Convention … were a Contracting State knowingly to surrender a fugitive to another State where there were substantial grounds for believing that he would be in danger of being subjected to torture, *however heinous the crime allegedly committed*"[49] [emphasis added]

However, the Court went on to observe that "inherent in the whole Convention is a search for a fair balance between the demands of the general interest of the community and the requirements of the protection of the individual's fundamental rights".[50] It noted further that the danger for a state obliged to harbour a fugitive was "a consideration which must be included among the factors to be taken into account in the interpretation and application of the notions of inhuman and degrading treatment or punishment in extradition cases".[51]

Unfortunately, the judgment does not fully explain what was meant by this comment. It is difficult to see how the notion of inhuman and degrading treatment anticipated in the state of destination can be interpreted by reference to the perceived danger to the expelling state of keeping the individual concerned on its territory. The Court was perhaps merely signifying that it did not seek to undermine the foundations of extradition and that it did not wish its judgment in *Soering* to be taken as a message to governments that they were obliged to harbour dangerous fugitives from justice unless both the risk of exposure and the threshold of severity tests were clearly met.

But this is quite different from taking the danger to the expelling state into account in assessing the dangers in the state of proposed destination.

The Court considered these comments again. In *Chahal*, the United Kingdom Government relied on Grotius' *De Iure Belli ac Pacis* to support the proposition that asylum is to be enjoyed by people "who suffer from undeserved enmity, not those who have done something that is injurious to human society or to other men".[52]

The Court rejected this argument, as the Commission had. It reaffirmed the absolute character, permitting no exception, of this provision which had been

---

49 *Soering v. the United Kingdom*, Application No. 14038/88, judgment of 7 July 1989, p. 26, paragraph 88.

50 Ibid., p. 27, paragraph 89.

51 Ibid.

52 *Chahal v. the United Kingdom*, Application No. 22414/93, report of 27 June 1995, p. 21, paragraph 98.

noted by the Court in *Vilvarajah*.[53] It found itself "unable to accept the government's submission that Article 3 of the Convention may have implied limitations entitling the State to expel a person because of the requirements of national security".[54] It stated:

> "The prohibition provided by Article 3 against ill-treatment is equally absolute in expulsion cases. Thus whenever substantial grounds have been shown for believing that an individual would face a real risk of being subjected to treatment contrary to Article 3 if removed to another State, the responsibility of the Contracting State to safeguard him or her against such treatment is engaged in the event of expulsion … In these circumstances, the activities of the individual in question, however undesirable or dangerous, cannot be a material consideration."[55]

The Court thus endorsed the Commission's view that:

> "While it is accepted that this may result in undesirable individuals finding a safe haven in a Contracting State, the Commission observes that the State is not without means of dealing with any threats posed thereby, the individual being subject to the ordinary criminal laws of the country concerned."

The protection afforded by Article 3 is thus wider than that provided by Articles 32 and 33 of the Geneva Convention.

In *Chahal*, the Court also considered the dicta in *Soering* quoted above. It held, in a somewhat Delphic comment, that:

> "[I]t should not be inferred from the Court's remarks concerning the risks of undermining the foundations of extradition … that there is any room for balancing the risk of ill-treatment against the reasons for expulsion in determining whether a state's responsibility under Article 3 is engaged."[56]

It did not, however, offer any suggestion as to what was to be inferred from the remarks.

The judgment in *Ahmed v. Austria*[57] was delivered some three weeks after that in *Chahal*. Mr Ahmed, a recognised refugee in Austria, was deprived of his Geneva Convention status because of criminal convictions and a residence ban was imposed on him. The Court found that, although it could not rule on whether the Austrian courts had correctly applied the Geneva Convention, the conditions in Somalia which had led to him being granted refugee status

---

53 *Vilvarajah and Others v. the United Kingdom*, Application Nos. 13163/87, 13164/87, 13165/87, 13447/87 and 13448/87, p. 34, paragraph 108.

54 *Chahal v. the United Kingdom*, Application No. 22414/93, report of 27 June 1995, p. 22, paragraph 102.

55 *Chahal v. the United Kingdom*, Application No. 22414/93, judgment of 15 November 1996, paragraph 80.

56 *Chahal v. the United Kingdom*, Application No. 22414/93, judgment of 15 November 1996, paragraph 81.

57 *Ahmed v. Austria*, Application No. 25964/94, judgment of 17 December 1996.

still prevailed and that his criminal convictions were therefore irrelevant to his need for protection from expulsion. The point seemed beyond dispute.[58]

In February 2005, for instance, in *Khashiyev and Akayera v. Russia,*[59] the Court held that terrorism will not justify a dilution of the prohibition on torture and inhuman and degrading treatment even "in the most difficult circumstances".

The *Ramzy Saadi* challenges

More recently, however, the Lithuanian, Portuguese and Slovakian Governments, together with, and at the instigation of, the United Kingdom, have intervened in the case of *Ramzy v. the Netherlands.*[60] They are attempting to persuade the Court to re-visit the decision in *Chahal* in the context of the perceived threat to national security posed by international terrorism. The applicant in *Ramzy* faces deportation to Algeria on the grounds of his suspected involvement in an Islamic extremist group in the Netherlands (although when charged with this offence he was acquitted). The case, and the interventions of various governments, raises issues of fundamental importance concerning the absolute nature of the prohibition on torture and other ill-treatment. The case for the Dutch Government had been that the applicant would not be exposed to a real risk of prohibited treatment on return. The intervening governments suggest that even if he would be exposed to such a risk it should be assessed in the light of the threat to security he posed. They suggest that the prohibition on return to face a real risk of absolutely prohibited treatment should no longer be absolute. The intervention of the four governments prompted ten international human rights non-governmental organisations to intervene also to challenge the United Kingdom's position. The case is still pending before the Court at the time of writing.

The EU Qualification Directive states in its preamble that its objective is to ensure common criteria for the identification of persons genuinely in need of international protection. Its text then goes on to exclude from the definition of a refugee entitled to protection it offers those who are excluded under the Geneva Convention. However, it also excludes from "subsidiary protection" those who are suspected of having committed criminal offences or of being a danger to the community (Article 17). As is clear from what has been written above, whether such individuals are suspected in this way, or even if they constitute a more substantiated threat, they still enjoy absolute protection from expulsion under the ECHR.

States need to be as aware of that overarching obligation as they are of the exclusion clauses of the Geneva Convention and the Qualification Directive.

---

58 See, for example, *R. v. the United Kingdom,* Application No. 28038/95, admissibility decision of 17 January 1997.

59 Applications Nos. 57942/00 and 57945/00, judgment of 24 February 2005.

60 *Ramzy v. the Netherlands,* Application No. 25424/05. See also *A. v. the Netherlands,* Application No. 4900/06. *Saadi v. Italy,* Application No. 37201/06, heard by the Grand Chamber on 11 July 2007, raised similar issues.

3. The risk of torture, inhuman or degrading treatment

For Article 3 of the Convention to be engaged, it must be shown that the applicant is at risk of treatment prohibited by that article.

The Qualification Directive (Article 15(b)) gives the right to EU "subsidiary protection" to those who are not at risk of persecution, but who are at risk of "torture or inhuman or degrading treatment or punishment ... in the country of origin".

Article 3 of the UNCAT prohibits expulsion to face torture.

The risk must be real. In *Thampibillai and Venkadajalasarma v. the Netherlands*[61] the Court observed that the applicant left Sri Lanka in 1994, almost four years after the killing of his father by the army and some three and a half years after he himself was arrested by the army and detained for two weeks. Therefore, since they found that it did not appear that these events constituted the reason for the applicant to flee his country[62] they relied on this finding to support their view that he was not therefore at a real risk on return.

In determining whether Article 3 is engaged, consideration must be given to what it is that is risked. The necessary threshold of severity must be met. In *Cruz Varas* the Court noted:

> "Ill-treatment must attain a minimum level of severity if it is to fall within the scope of Article 3. The assessment of this minimum is, in the nature of things, relative; it depends on all the circumstances of the case."[63]

Citing these dicta with approval in *Vilvarajah v. the United Kingdom,* the Court went on to add:

> "The Court's examination of the existence of a risk of ill-treatment in breach of Article 3 at the relevant time must necessarily be a rigorous one in view of the absolute character of this provision and the fact that it enshrines one of the fundamental values of the democratic societies making up the Council of Europe."[64]

For those who are not victims of persecution as defined in the Geneva Convention, the risk of acts of physical torture, or of inhuman and degrading treatment is the most commonly invoked ground.

In *Said v. the Netherlands*[65] the applicant was a deserter from the Ethiopian Army whose expulsion would have violated Article 3 as he risked being punished

---

61 *Thampibillai and Venkadajalasarma v. the Netherlands,* Application No. 61350/00, judgment of 17 February 2004.

62 Cf. the approach of the UNCAT: footnotes 109, 110 below.

63 *Cruz Varas v. Sweden,* Application No. 15576/89, judgment of 20 March 1991, paragraph 83.

64 *Vilvarajah and Others v. the United Kingdom,* Application Nos. 13163/87, 13164/87 and 13165/87, judgment of 30 October 1991, paragraph 108.

65 Application No. 2345/02, judgment of 15 July 2005.

by, *inter alia*, being tied up in prolonged exposure to the sun in very high temperatures. In *Jabari v. Turkey*[66] an Iranian woman who had committed adultery argued successfully that were the Turkish authorities to expel her to Iran, she would be exposed to treatment contrary to Article 3 in the form of whipping, flogging and stoning on account of her extramarital affair.

As noted above, the first ever decision of the Court in the case of *Soering* concerned the risk of facing the psychological distress of being subject to the death row phenomenon if extradited to stand trial in the USA. The Court found that this risk reached the necessary level of severity.

The effect of expulsion on the medical condition of the applicant has also been considered. For such claims to succeed, the circumstances of the particular case must be exceptional, such as those found in *D. v. the United Kingdom*.[67] That case concerned the proposed expulsion of a person in the terminal stages of Aids to a country where he had no family or material resources, where there was no social welfare provision available to him and no treatment for Aids. The Court found a violation of Article 3 because his actual removal from the hospital bed where he was dying engaged that article as well as his imminent deterioration and death in conditions of destitution that would have awaited him on return.

However, three recent subsequent decisions have found inadmissible cases where the HIV-positive patients argued that their forcible return to Tanzania, Togo and Zambia respectively would expose them to treatment contrary to Article 3.[68] None was found to reach the threshold set by *D. v. the United Kingdom*. It appears that an applicant must have reached the advanced stage of Aids or suffer from HIV-related illness. Furthermore, if treatment is available in the country of origin, albeit at a considerable cost, the Court is reluctant to find Article 3 engaged.

In *Hukić v. Sweden*[69] the Court considered a complaint alleging that the expulsion of a 5 year-old boy with Down's syndrome from Sweden to Bosnia and Herzegovina, where the care he would receive would fall far short of that which he was presently enjoying in Sweden, would violate Article 3. The Court found the case inadmissible.

---

66 *Jabari v. Turkey*, Application No. 40035/98, judgment of 11 July 2000.

67 *D. v. the United Kingdom*, Application No. 30240/96, judgment of 2 May 1997.

68 *Ndangoya v. Sweden*, Application No. 17868/03, decision of 22 June 2004, *Amegnigan v. the Netherlands*, Application No. 25629/04, decision of 25 November 2004, and *S.C.C. v. Sweden*, Application No. 46553/99, decision of 15 February 2002.

69 *Hukić v. Sweden*, Application No. 17416/05, decision of 27 September 2005.

Psychiatric patients at risk of expulsion have also, albeit unsuccessfully, advanced arguments under Article 3.[70] In *Bensaid v. the United Kingdom*[71] the applicant was a schizophrenic suffering from a psychotic illness and feared treatment contrary to Article 3 should he be returned to Algeria. The Court considered that the suffering associated with an illness could, in principle, fall within the scope of Article 3 but the exceptional circumstances found in *D. v. the United Kingdom* were lacking.

The personal nature of the risk

The United Kingdom Government in *Vilvarajah* argued:

> "The consequences of finding a breach of Article 3 in the present case would be that all other persons in similar situations facing random risks on account of civil turmoil in the State where they lived would be entitled not to be removed, thereby permitting the entry of a potentially very large class of people with the attendant serious social and economic consequences."[72]

In practice, and perhaps to alleviate those concerns, the approach of the Court has been highly cautious. The Court is silently conscious of the fact that the Strasbourg system of supervision needs to retain the fullest possible support and compliance of the contracting parties if it is to be at all effective.

In *Vilvarajah* the Court agreed with the United Kingdom Government that the evidence did not show that the applicants' position was any worse than the generality of other young male members of the Tamil community returning to their country. "A mere possibility of ill-treatment, however, in such circumstances, is not in itself sufficient to give rise to a breach of Article 3."[73] It found no breach of Article 3 despite the fact that the applicants, who had been returned to Sri Lanka before the case was examined by the Commission and Court, had in fact been subjected to treatment contrary to Article 3 on their return. The reason given by the Court in exculpating the United Kingdom

---

70 *Ovdienko v. Finland*, Application No. 1383/4, decision of 31 June 2005, *Bensaid v. the United Kingdom* (Schizophrenia), Application No. 44599/98, judgment of 6 February 2001.

71 Application No. 44599/98, judgment of 6 February 2001.

72 Compare Article 2, OAU 1969 Refugees Convention 1000 UNTS 46, which expressly covers such situations: "The term refugee shall also apply to every person who, owing to external aggression, occupation, foreign domination or events seriously disturbing public order in either part or the whole of his country of origin or nationality is compelled to leave his place of habitual residence in order to seek refuge in another place outside his country of origin or nationality."

73 See *Vilvarajah and Others v. the United Kingdom*, Applications Nos. 13163/87, 13164/87 and 13165/87, judgment of 30 October 1991, paragraph 111.

Government was that "there existed no special distinguishing features in their cases that could or should have enabled the Secretary of State to foresee that they would be treated in this way".

The United Kingdom's own independent asylum appeal tribunal (which was only able to consider the appeal against the refusal of asylum on the merits after the applicants had been removed) had had no difficulty in deciding that asylum had been wrongly refused. The Strasbourg Court was not persuaded, even by the finding of that tribunal, that the government had erred. (The Commission, when considering the same case, had been evenly divided as to whether there was a breach or not – the President's casting vote being required to find no breach.)

It is difficult to reconcile the absolute nature of the protection offered by Article 3 with the view that an individual must show not just that he or she is at real risk of prohibited treatment but that he or she is relatively more at real risk of prohibited treatment than others in similar vulnerable circumstances. However, the same approach was adopted in 2005 to returns to Iraq (see *Muslim v. Turkey*[74] below).

The judgment in *Salah Sheekh* has now revisited the approach taken in *Vilvarajah*. Finding, as had the Dutch Government, that the applicant and his family belonged to a targeted minority, the Court stated:

> "it cannot be required of the applicant that he establishes that further special distinguishing features, concerning him personally, exist in order to show that he was, and continues to be, personally at risk. ... it might render the protection offered [by Article3] illusory if, in addition to the fact that he belongs to the Ashraf ... the applicant be required to show the existence of further special distinguishing features."[75]

The Qualification Directive includes in its definition of "serious harm" the risk of which entitles individuals to subsidiary protection "serious and individual threat to a civilian's life or person by reason of indiscriminate violence in situations of international or internal armed conflict" (Article 15c).

It is difficult to see how the concept of "individual threat" by reason of violence which is "indiscriminate" is not inherently contradictory, or why only threats to civilians are covered (see, for example, *Said v. the Netherlands*, above) and whether these provisions, if relied on to exclude an individual from protection, would be considered compatible with the Convention standards set out in *Salah Sheekh*.

The Committee against Torture applies the test of "personal, present, foreseeable, and real" risk (see page 51 below).

---

74 Application No. 53566/99, judgment of 26 April 2005.

75 *Salah Sheekh v. the Netherlands*, Application No. 1948/04, judgment of 13 January 2007, paragraph 148.

Time of assessing risk

A "present" risk

The passing of time has been held by the Court to erase, or reduce to a negligible level, a risk that may once have existed.

The Geneva Convention (Article 1C) and the EU Qualification Directive (Article 11) both include "cessation clauses" which preclude protection under their provisions when circumstances have sufficiently improved.

The case of *Said v. the Netherlands*[76] demonstrated an ongoing risk. The applicant alleged to have deserted the Eritrean army, and maintained that, in the current climate in Eritrea, he still ran a real risk of being subjected to treatment proscribed by Article 3 on account both of his criticism of the military and of his desertion:

> "Since the nature of the Contracting States' responsibility under Article 3 in cases of this kind lies in the act of exposing an individual to the risk of ill-treatment, the existence of the risk must be assessed primarily with reference to those facts which were known or ought to have been known to the Contracting State at the time of the expulsion (see *Vilvarajah and Others v. the United Kingdom*, 30 October 1991, Series A no. 215, p. 36, § 107, and *H.L.R. v. France*, cited above, p. 758, § 37). In the present case, given that the applicant has not yet been expelled, the material point in time is that of the Court's consideration of the case. Even though the historical position is of interest in so far as it may shed light on the current situation and its likely evolution, it is the present conditions which are decisive and it is therefore necessary to take into account information that has come to light after the final decision taken by the domestic authorities (see *Chahal v. the United Kingdom*, judgment of 15 November 1996, pp. 1856 and 1859, §§ 86 and 97, *Reports* 1996-V, and *H.L.R. v. France*, cited above)."[77]

In *Tomic v. the United Kingdom*[78] a majority of the Chamber rejected the application of an ethnic Serb who alleged that his return to Croatia would put him at risk. The Court dismissed his claim as manifestly ill-founded and attached importance to the fact that the hostilities had ceased and Croatia was now a party to the ECHR.

In *Hida v. Denmark*[79] the applicant, a Kosovan, alleged that his forced return to Kosovo would subject him to treatment in violation of Article 3. Taking into account the general situation in Kosovo at the time (2004), the Court noted that incidents of violence and crimes against minorities continued to be a cause for concern and that the need remained for international protection of members of ethnic minority communities. However, despite this cause for

---

76 *Said v. the Netherlands*, cited above.

77 *Said v. the Netherlands*, cited above, paragraph 48.

78 Application No. 17837/03, decision of 14 October 2003.

79 *Hida v. Denmark*, Application No. 38025/02, decision of 19 February 2004.

concern, forced returns to Kosovo were taking place subject to an individu-alised screening process performed by UNMIK. The Court noted that Denmark had already presented to UNMIK a number of Kosovans whose applications for a residence permit in Denmark had been refused, following which they were forced to leave the country. In some cases, UNMIK objected to the return of the persons in which case the Danish suspended their return until further notice. In the applicant's case this "safety" process of individualised screening also applied, that is, in the event that UNMIK objected to his return, it would be suspended until further notice. The Court therefore found no substantial grounds for believing that the applicant, an ethnic Roma, would face a real and present risk of being subjected to treatment contrary to Article 3. (The EU Qualification Directive (Article 7) specifically provides that protection can be provided, *inter alia*, by international organisations.)

In *Muslim v. Turkey*[80] the applicant (whose application had been lodged in 1999) had alleged that if sent back to Iraq he would face execution by the authorities of the former regime that held him responsible for an attack against a member of the Baath party who was close to Saddam Hussein. Having regard to the conditions in Iraq when the complaint was considered in 2005, the Court came to the conclusion that the applicant no longer faced the same level of risk. The Court reaffirmed the principle that a mere "possibility" of ill-treatment on account of the unsettled general situation in a country is in itself insufficient to give rise to a breach of Article 3 of the Convention.[81]

Where the threatened removal has not yet occurred

Where applicants have not yet been deported, a finding of the Court in their favour will not be that the decision to expel them was a violation but only that it would be a violation of the Convention were the expulsion or extradi-tion to go ahead.

In *Chahal* and *Ahmed* the Court noted "the material point in time must be that of the Court's consideration of the case"[82] and not the time at which the decision to remove was made.

The Court in both cases went on to state: "Although the historical position is of interest in so far as it may shed light on the current situation and its likely evolution, it is the present conditions which are decisive."[83]

---

80 *Muslim v. Turkey*, Application No. 53566/99, judgment of 26 April 2005.

81 See for further information *Katani and Others v. Germany*, Application No. 67679/01, judgment of 31 May 2001.

82 *Chahal v. the United Kingdom*, Application No. 22414/93, judgment of 15 November 1996, paragraph 86.

83 Ibid.

The correct point in time for assessing whether there is a real risk to the applicant by a proposed expulsion is the time when the Court considers the case. The *present* conditions are decisive (see *F. v. the United Kingdom*).[84]

The Court will therefore take into account information that has come to light after the final decision taken by domestic authorities, but before it has considered the case. This may mean that the Court is revisiting the decision to expel months or even years (cf. *Muslim v. Turkey* above) after it has been taken in the light of any changes in circumstances, particularly conditions in the country of proposed destination, which have occurred in the interim. If the situation is held to have ameliorated sufficiently since the application was brought to the Court, the finding will be, as in *Muslim,* of no violation.

Where a final decision to expel has not been carried out, and all domestic remedies to overturn it have failed, it will usually have been because the government has complied with the temporary measures indicated by the European Court under Rule 39 of its Rules of Procedure (previously Rule 36; see below at pages 124 *et seq*). Since the approach of the Court is that a violation of the Convention only occurs when there is an act of expulsion rather than when there is a final decision to expel, it is immaterial that the expulsion would have violated Article 3 had it gone ahead as a result of the domestic authorities' final decision had the European Court not intervened.

This approach may not be entirely consistent with the obligation contained in Article 1 to "secure" the Convention rights[85] in domestic law and practice since it is clear that the individuals would have been expelled (and therefore presumably also ill-treated) but for the intervention of the Convention organs. It is difficult to sustain the argument that the state has discharged its obligations to "secure" the domestic protection of an absolute right for a vulnerable individual if an absolutely prohibited expulsion is only prevented by recourse to the European Court.

Where the applicants have already been expelled

In the *Cruz Varas* judgment of 20 March 1991 the Court noted the following principles as being relevant to the assessment of the risk of ill-treatment:

"Since the nature of the Contracting States' responsibility under Article 3 in cases of this kind lies in the act of exposing an individual to the risk of ill-treatment, the existence of the risk must be assessed primarily with reference to those facts which were known or ought to have been known to the Contracting State *at the time of the expulsion*; the Court is not precluded, however, from having regard to information which comes to light subsequent to the expulsion. This may be of value in

---

84 *F. v. the United Kingdom*, Application No. 17341/03, decision of 22 June 2004.

85 The English text uses the word "secure". The French text uses the word "*reconnaissent*".

confirming or refuting the appreciation that has been made by the Contracting Party of the well-foundedness or otherwise of an applicant's fears."[86] [emphasis added]

In *Mamatkulov and Askarov v. Turkey* the applicants were expelled to Uzbekistan, despite the making of a Rule 39 indication to the contrary by the Court (see below for the procedures before the ECtHR). The Grand Chamber held that the risk had to be assessed at the date of the actual extradition of the applicants. In *Mamatkulov* the majority of the Grand Chamber concluded that there was insufficient evidence to support a finding that the Turkish Government should have been aware *at the time of the extradition* of the existence of a real risk that ill-treatment in breach of Article 3 would occur. In *Mamatkulov* it was nevertheless stated that where an applicant has already been extradited "the Court is not precluded from having regard to information which comes to light subsequent to the extradition".[87]

Despite its clear repetition of the principle that the assessment must be of the risk at the date of the expulsion, the majority did not consider that they had to be satisfied that the applicants had not suffered ill-treatment which they feared. They relied rather on the absence of concrete evidence that the ill-treatment feared had actually occurred. The applicants' representatives before the Court had been unable to receive any further communications from their clients after the extradition had taken place. The Court considered that this absence of evidence supported their finding that there was no real risk of which the Turkish Government should have been aware at the time of the removal. The joint (partly dissenting) opinion disagreed with the majority that the lack of evidence of ill-treatment after the return to Uzbekistan was a relevant factor to assessing the well-foundedness of the risk of which the Turkish Government should have been aware at the time of the extradition. (The Grand Chamber did, however, find a violation of Article 34 because of the failure to comply with the Rule 39 indication.)

In *Vilvarajah*, the applicants were expelled and there was undisputed evidence that they were ill-treated in Sri Lanka. Their return to the United Kingdom was subsequently ordered by the United Kingdom courts, which held that they had been wrongly refused asylum. The European Court nevertheless found no violation of Article 3 as – despite the finding of the United Kingdom courts that they had been wrongly refused asylum – the United Kingdom executive authorities could not, apparently, have foreseen that they would in fact be ill-treated in the manner which they had claimed.

---

86 *Cruz Varas v. Sweden*, Application No. 15576/89, judgment of 20 March 1991, paragraph 76.

87 *Mamatkulov and Askarov v. Turkey*, Applications Nos. 46827/99 and 46951/99, judgment of 4 February 2005.

Internal flight alternative

In *Chahal v. the United Kingdom,* the United Kingdom Government argued that even if the Court were to find that the applicant would be at risk in the Punjab he would be safe in other areas of India. The Court found that although the applicant was at particular risk in Punjab he was not safe elsewhere in India either.

In *Hilal v. the United Kingdom,* the government alleged that even assuming the applicant was at risk in Zanzibar the situation in mainland Tanzania was more secure. The Court found, as they had in *Chahal,* that human rights abuses were also prevalent in the areas of Tanzania other than Zanzibar. As in *Chahal,* the police could not be relied on as a safeguard against arbitrary acts and the applicant was at risk of being moved to an area where he would be at risk.

The recent judgment in *Salah Sheekh* examines the question of the internal flight alternative in some detail. The applicant came from Somalia, where he was a member of the Ashraf minority. The Dutch Government recognised that some parts of Somalia were unsafe and did not return people to those parts. However, it considered other areas to be safe enough to justify returns. The applicant alleged that, as a member of his minority group without clan support, he would be unprotected even in those areas, and thus was not only at risk there, but also at risk of being forced into the areas which were recognised as being unsafe. The Court agreed, citing its earlier judgments in *Chahal* and *Hilal,* as well as the admissibility decision in *T.I.,* which it found applicable by analogy. The Court stated:

> "as a pre-condition for relying on an internal flight alternative, certain guarantees have to be in place: the person to be expelled must be able to travel to the area concerned, to gain admittance and be able to settle there, failing which an issue under Article 3 may arise, the more so if in the absence of such guarantees there is a possibility of the expellee ending up in a part of the country of origin where he or she may be subjected to ill-treatment".[88]

The evaluation of the risk

The Court, and the Commission before it, have been understandably reluctant to find that applicants have discharged the burden of proof which rests on them in the face of findings of insufficient risk, or lack of credibility, by experienced and well-informed governments. The principles which it clearly recites in the jurisprudence will more rarely result in a finding of a violation on the facts.

Many cases are rejected at the admissibility level because the Court is inclined to attach more weight to the government's assessment of the situation than the applicant's fears. It thus does not avail itself of the opportunity to examine the merits of the case.

---

88 *Salah Sheekh v. the Netherlands,* Application No. 1948/04, judgment of 13 January 2007, paragraph 141.

The approach in European Convention on Human Rights jurisprudence until recently had been for the Convention organs to reiterate that the governments who may examine thousands of asylum applications from a given country in any year, and who have access to information through their overseas diplomatic posts, are in principle best placed to assess the situation which prevails in the country of origin or proposed destination.[89]

The Court will consider all relevant evidence. In *X v. the Federal Republic of Germany*,[90] for example, it found that the behaviour of the applicant provided a good indication of whether he truly considered himself to be in real danger.

Nevertheless, the Court considers that there is a positive duty on the national authorities, if the need arises, to go beyond the evidence provided by the applicant and to use diverse sources of current information in order to gain a clearer understanding of the situation in the receiving country, as in *Katani and Others v. Germany*.[91] Furthermore, the Court will have regard to the authenticity of the documents as well as the legitimacy and credibility of an applicant's claims. In *V. Matsiukhina and A. Matsiukhin v. Sweden*[92] the Court acknowledged that, due to the special situation in which asylum seekers often find themselves, it is frequently necessary to give them the benefit of the doubt when it comes to assessing the credibility of their statements and the documents submitted in support thereof. However, when information is presented which gives strong reasons to question the veracity of an asylum seeker's submissions, the individual must provide a satisfactory explanation for the alleged inaccuracies in those submissions.[93]

In order for the Court to evaluate the level of risk, it has stated that it is incumbent on persons who allege that their expulsion would amount to a breach of Article 3 to adduce, to the greatest extent practically possible, "material information allowing the authorities of the Contracting State concerned, as well as the Court, to assess the risk a removal may entail". The EU Qualification Directive imposes similar obligations. In determining whether substantial grounds have been shown for believing the existence of a real risk of treatment

---

89 See the judgments of the Court and reports of the Commission in *Vijayanathan and Pusparajah v. France*, Applications Nos. 17550/90 and 17825/90, judgment of 27 August 1992, *Cruz Varas v. Sweden*, Application No. 15576/89, judgment of 20 March 1991, and many unpublished admissibility decisions. As late as 1997 the Commission was rejecting claims from Kosovan Albanians that they were at risk from Milosevic's regime in Serbia. See *Haliti v. Germany*, Application No. 31182/96, decision of 3 December 1997, *Tahiri v. Sweden*, decision of 11 January 1995, Application No. 25129/94, *R.B. v. Sweden*, Application No. 22508/93, decision of 21 October 1993.

90 *X v. the Federal Republic of Germany*, DR 5, p. 137.

91 *Katani and Others v. Germany*, Application No. 67679/01, decision of 31 May 2001.

92 *V. Matsiukhina and A. Matsiukhin v. Sweden*, Application No. 31260/04, decision of 21 June 2005.

93 Cf. case law of the UNCAT, below pp. 49 *et seq.*

contrary to Article 3 the Court will assess the issue in the light of all the material placed before it or, if necessary, "material obtained *ex proprio motu*".[94] In *Said v. the Netherlands*, for example, the Court expressly rejected the respondent government's finding that the applicant lacked credibility.

The report of the Commission in *Chahal* marked a departure from the Commission's earlier approach to the government's assessment of the situation in the country of destination. The Commission was impressed by the evidence submitted by the applicants as to the situation in India.

On the basis of the material before it the Court also found that the applicants would be at risk. They were unable to find in the material provided by the respondent government "any solid evidence that the police are now under democratic control or that the judiciary has been able fully to reassert its own independent authority in the Punjab". In particular they noted the views of the United Nations Special Rapporteur on Torture and dismissed the assurances given by the Indian Government to the United Kingdom Government as not providing an adequate guarantee of safety. In *Bahaddar*[95] the Commission had expressed the view that expulsion to Bangladesh would be a violation of Article 3, although the Court did not rule on the point since the claim was rejected for failure to exhaust domestic remedies. In *T.I.* (a case about a return under the Dublin Convention of a Sri Lankan whose asylum claim had been rejected in Germany),[96] the Court expressed its concerns that the applicant would be at risk if returned to Sri Lanka although the German courts had rejected his claims as (*inter alia*) lacking credibility.

In *Hatami v. Sweden*[97] the Commission also substituted its own evaluation of the evidence for that of the Swedish authorities, finding that the applicant's claim to have been tortured was credible, that the Swedish authorities had placed reliance on a ten minute interview conducted without effective interpretation, and that they had reached their decision on an incorrect interpretation of the available facts. In *Hatami* the Commission for the first time echoed (without express reference) the case law of the United Nations Committee against Torture to the effect that "complete accuracy is seldom to be expected from victims of torture".[98]

The Court will sometimes use the interventions of third parties in order to provide a more holistic view of the situation in particular countries,[99] and

---

94 *Cruz Varas v. Sweden*, Application No. 15576/89, judgment of 20 March 1991, paragraph 75.

95 *Bahaddar v. the Netherlands*, Application No. 25894/94, judgment of 19 February 1998.

96 *T.I. v. the United Kingdom*, Application No. 43844/98, judgment of 7 March 2000.

97 *Hatami v. Sweden*, Application No. 32448/96, judgment of 23 April 1998.

98 Ibid.

99 *Mamatkulov and Askarov v. Turkey*, Applications Nos. 4627/99 and 46951/99, judgment of 4 February 2005.

exceptionally, members of the Court will occasionally make field trips as delegates in order to make factual assessments and assess credibility.[100] The Court will very often rely on country reports and publications of national governments and international organisations. In *Said v. the Netherlands*[101] a US Department of State Country Report was used by the Court to assess human rights conditions in Eritrea. The separate opinion of Cypriot Judge Loucaides contains a scathing attack on the inclusion of a US Government report in the judgment, considering it an unreliable product of a non-independent, non-impartial political government agency, by reference to an earlier US report that he considered grossly failed to acknowledge human rights violations in Cyprus.

In *Salah Sheekh* the Court noted:[102]

> "The Court will assess the issues in the light of all the material placed before it, or, if necessary obtained proprio motu, in particular where the applicant – or a third party within the meaning of Article 36 of the Convention – provides reasoned grounds which cast doubt on the accuracy of the information relied on by the respondent Government … It must be satisfied that the assessment is adequate and sufficiently supported by domestic material as well as by materials originating from other reliable and objective sources such as, for instance other Contracting or non-contracting states, agencies of the United Nations and reputable non-governmental organisations. In its supervisory task under Article 19 of the Convention, it would be too narrow an approach under Article 3 … if the Court, as an international human rights court, were only to take into account materials made available by the domestic authorities of the state concerned without comparing these with materials from other reliable and objective sources."

Diplomatic assurances and the real risk test

Some states are increasingly seeking to rely on recourse to diplomatic assurances either in the course of establishing that the real risk test is not met, or if it is met that it can somehow be displaced by reliance on such assurances.

At the most simple level assurances can clearly have a role to play. Where an expulsion or extradition might expose an individual to the death penalty, an undertaking by the receiving state that the death penalty will not be sought or carried out may be sufficient to negate the risk if the receiving state is one whose word is reliable, whose legal system enables such undertakings to be binding, and whose past conduct and respect for the rule of law confirms that they are both willing and, as importantly, able to assure that its assurances are valid.

Unfortunately recourse to diplomatic assurances is increasingly being had in cases where the state of proposed destination meets none of those criteria. In

---

100 *N. v. Finland*, Application No. 38885/02, judgment of 26 February 2005.

101 *Said v. the Netherlands*, Application No. 2345/02, judgment of 15 June 2005.

102 *Salah Sheek v. the Netherlands*, Application No. 1948/04, judgment of 13 January 2007, paragraph 136.

Chahal the United Kingdom Government sought to rely on assurances given by the Indian authorities. The Court found that the Indian Government had made the assurances in good faith, but that violations of human rights by members of the security forces in the Punjab remained a "recalcitrant and enduring problem", despite the efforts of the government to bring about reform. The assurances were therefore insufficient to displace the risk.

The situation was somewhat different in *Mamatkulov*. There it was the government itself which was the well-documented persistent author of gross and systematic violations of human rights. The majority in *Mamatkulov* found that the assurances given by the Uzbek Government were sufficient to negate the existence of a real risk. The Turkish Government had relied on Uzbek undertakings that the applicants' property would not be subject to general confiscation nor would they be subjected to torture or the death penalty. The minority[103] disagreed. They found that the Turkish Government's reliance on the assurances of the Uzbek regime did not dispel the existence of the real risk. They considered that the undisputed findings concerning the general widespread human rights abuses in Uzbekistan and the applicants' specific situation as members of a particularly at-risk group who had been charged with terrorist attacks on the president himself were sufficient to support the finding of a real risk.

Since the judgment in *Mamatkulov* other organs of the Council of Europe have also commented on the use of diplomatic assurances. The Commissioner for Human Rights wrote in June 2006 that diplomatic assurances from states with a track record of torture:

> "are not credible and have also turned out to be ineffective in well documented cases. The governments have already violated binding international norms and it is plain wrong to subject anyone to the risk of torture on the basis of an even less solemn undertaking to make an exception in an individual case".

The recent report of the Parliamentary Assembly of the Council of Europe on extraordinary renditions and secret detentions concludes that "relying on the principle of trust and assurances given by undemocratic states known not to respect human rights is simply cowardly and hypocritical".

The European Committee for the Prevention of Torture's (CPT) 15th Report has echoed this approach: "Fears are growing that the use of diplomatic assurances is in fact circumventing the prohibition of torture and ill-treatment."

The CPT focuses on the absence of any practical mechanisms for monitoring compliance:

> "To have any chance of being effective, such a mechanism would certainly need to incorporate some key guarantees, including the right of independent and suitably qualified persons to visit the individual concerned at any time without prior notice and to interview him/her in private in a place of their choosing."

---

103 These dissenting judges were Judges Bratza, Bonello and Hedigan.

The approach of the Group of Specialists on Human Rights and the Fight against Terrorism (DH-S-TER) is similarly pragmatic.[104]

The recent case of *Salah Sheekh* did not concern diplomatic assurances as such, but the Court took the opportunity to note that the Dutch Government lacked any mechanism for monitoring whether or not the area to which it proposed sending the applicant would prove safe in reality for him once expelled.

In the final analysis, however, it is only the Court which has the power to rule on whether the diplomatic assurances offered in any particular case are sufficiently reliable to ensure that the expelling state has complied with the absolute prohibition on expulsion to face a real risk of prohibited treatment. The *Ramzy* case, discussed above in relation to exclusion from protection, also raises issues about diplomatic assurances on which the Court may eventually be required to rule in the near future.

The approach taken by the UNCAT committee to diplomatic assurances is discussed at page 52 below. The UNHCR adopted a note on diplomatic assurances in August 2006,[105] and the UN General Assembly also recognised that diplomatic assurances do not release states from their obligations – in particular the principle of *non-refoulement*.[106]

"Safe" countries

As regards the material scope of the Geneva Convention it is well settled that there is no distinct right to be granted asylum, only to be protected from *refoulement* to a place where one would be at risk. Article 33, paragraph 1, of the Geneva Convention, in parallel to Article 3 of the European Convention on Human Rights, establishes only the principle that requires contracting states to refrain from expelling or returning refugees to territories where their lives or freedom would be threatened. It follows that there is, in principle, no prohibition on the return of a refugee to a country in which he will be safe, however reluctant he may be to go there.[107]

---

104 See Final Activity Report of the DH-S-TER on diplomatic assurances (extracts from 62nd meeting report of the CDDH), in particular paragraphs 20-21. Available at: www.coe.int/t/e/human_rights/cddh/3._committees01.%20steering%20 committee%20for%20human%20rights%20(cddh)/06.%20activity%20reports /2006/dh-s-ter.asp#P33_4961

105 www.unhcr.org/cgi-bin/texis/vtx/home/opendoc.pdf?tbl+RSDLEGAL&id+44dc81164

106 UN Doc A/C.3/60/L.25/Rev.1. See also the warning of the UN Special Rapporteur against Torture, UN press release, 23 August 2005.

107 See *Rosenberg v. Yee Chien Woo*, 402 United States 49 (1970) (US Supreme Court); and *Hurt v. Minister of Manpower and Immigration* (1978), 2 C.F. 340 (Canadian Federal Court of Appeal).

The concept of a "safe" country can arise in a number of contexts. Either the state where applicants claim to be at risk is considered safe, or the applicants are being sent to a so-called "safe third country" but fear that they will be removed onward to the country where they fear ill-treatment, or the conditions of onward return will violate Article 3.[108]

Asylum seekers whose country of origin is generally deemed to be free of persecution are often returned there, frequently without substantive consideration of their individual circumstances. The asylum applications of individuals from such "safe" countries are generally subjected to consideration under an accelerated procedure. Individuals can sometimes even be refused leave to enter the country where they are trying to seek asylum.[109]

Expulsion to EU states and ECHR contracting parties

The Qualification Directive refers only to "third country nationals" and thus excludes from its application anyone who is a citizen of an EU state even if they would otherwise be in need of protection. The Protocol on Asylum for Nationals of Member States of the European Union as annexed to the Treaty Establishing the European Community provides that "Member States shall be regarded as constituting safe countries of origin in respect of each other for all legal and practical purposes in relation to asylum matters".[110] Under the protocol, applications for asylum from nationals of a member state generally may not be considered.

The case of *Irruretagoyena v. France*[111] concerned an ETA member who feared reprisals from the Spanish police on his return. His application for a Rule 36 (now Rule 39) indication was refused and he was handed over to the Spanish police, who subjected him to ill-treatment including the administration of electric shocks. His complaint was rejected, *inter alia*, because the CPT had recently reported a diminution of the well-documented practices of the Spanish police contrary to Article 3 and it did not therefore consider that at the time of his expulsion there were serious reasons for believing that he would be submitted to the ill-treatment which he subsequently suffered. The Commission also noted, however, that he could bring a complaint against Spain in relation

---

108 This was the case in the complaints relating to expulsions from Lampedusa to Libya in *Hussun and Others v. Italy* (Application No. 10175/05 and others) which were declared admissible on 11 May 2006.

109 Lambert, *Seeking asylum: Comparative law and practice in selected European countries*, Martinus Nijhoff Publishers, Dordrecht, 1995, pp. 89-90.

110 Protocol on Asylum for Nationals of Member States of the European Union, annexed to the Treaty of Amsterdam.

111 Application No. 32829/96, decision of 12 January 1998. See also *Urrutikoetxea v. France*, Application No. 31113/96, decision of 5 December 1996.

to the torture which he suffered at the hands of the police on his return.[112] The Court noted that he had not made an asylum application in France. It did not note that this was unnecessary since, as he was an EEA national, he had a directly effective right to reside in France under EU law.

In *Tomic v. the United Kingdom*,[113] the Court considered it significant that the state (Croatia) to which the ethnic Serb applicant was being returned was a party to the ECHR which had accepted the obligation to provide procedural guarantees and effective remedies in respect of breaches of the ECHR.

Expulsion to "safe third countries"

The practice of returning asylum seekers to a "safe third country", that is, a state other than the one where the individual claims to be at risk of prohibited treatment, has been common in European states since the 1980s. During the 1990s it was applied more systematically, and has been incorporated into the national asylum legislation of most western European countries. It forms a major plank in the construction of international co-operation, particularly within the European Union.

As a result of the adoption of the Dublin Convention (now the "Dublin Regulation") and a phalanx of bilateral readmission agreements, many states are now sending people back, not directly to the state where they fear ill-treatment, but to a state which may then expel them onwards to that state.[114]

In *T.I. v. the United Kingdom*[115] the Court considered that state responsibility could arise by sending an asylum seeker to a third country under the provisions of the Dublin Convention (now the Dublin Regulation see page 133) if, in the circumstances, there was a real risk that the applicant would be sent on to a country where he faced treatment contrary to Article 3.

---

112 It would be unfortunate if the findings of the CPT that states had reduced the number of violations of Article 3 were to be used to deprive individuals of the absolute protection which that article affords. The same concerns apply, *mutatis mutandis*, to the friendly settlement adopted on 5 April 2000 in the *Denmark v. Turkey* inter-state case which records the advances that Turkey has made in improving the training of police and increasing the penalties for violations of Article 3. Whilst these advances are to be welcomed and encouraged, they should not be invoked to exculpate any future violations which occur either in the countries themselves or by the states expelling individuals to those countries.

113 Application No. 17837/03, decision of 14 October 2003.

114 See European Parliament working paper "Asylum in the EU Member States", LIBE 108, January 2000.

115 *T.I. v. the United Kingdom*, Application No. 43844/98, judgment of 7 March 2000.

There are two fundamental potential dangers for the asylum seeker inherent in the "safe third country" concept. The first is that they will be "bounced" back and forth from one alleged "safe third country" to another, as successive states refuse to examine their application substantively. Whilst not contravening any express provision of the Geneva Convention, this practice raises serious issues under the European Convention on Human Rights. The Commission has considered the problem of "refugees in orbit" under Article 3:

> "Under certain circumstances the repeated expulsion of a foreigner without identity papers or travel documents and whose state of origin is unknown or refuses to accept him could raise a problem under Article 3 of the Convention which prohibits inhuman or degrading treatment."[116]

The United Nations High Commissioner for Refugees (UNHCR) sees such practices as contrary to the premise that:

> "an asylum seeker cannot be removed to a third country in order that he apply for asylum there, *unless that country agrees to admit him to its territory as an asylum seeker and consider his request*".[117] [emphasis added]

Concerns have also been raised that some Council of Europe member states, which are generally deemed to be safe third countries, are not necessarily safe for certain types of asylum seeker because of the lack of a harmonised approach and consistency of procedural safeguards. For example, Austrian law did not protect deserters, or conscientious objectors, even if they faced the death penalty in their home state, while civil war victims who cited subjection to arbitrary arrest, torture or rape as reasons for being granted asylum could be turned down.[118] As late as 1997, Kosovan Albanians who feared serving in Milosevic's army were refused asylum in Germany.[119] This lack of consistency was one of the concerns leading to the adoption of the Qualification Directive which should lead to more consistent criteria being adopted by EU states.

The second danger is that, in a process of "chain removal", the asylum seeker is ultimately expelled from one country to the next and back to his or her country of origin without a substantive examination (or re-examination) of his or her claim. On this issue the United Nations High Commissioner for Refugees has written:

> "The policy whereby an asylum seeker arriving from a so-called 'safe third country' is returned to that country without his substantive claim having been considered

---

116 *X v. the Federal Republic of Germany*, Application No. 8100/77, not reported. See further *Giama v. Belgium*, Application No. 7612/76, *Yearbook* 23 (1980), p. 428.

117 *The "safe third country" policy in the light of the international obligations of countries* vis-à-vis *refugees and asylum seekers*, UNHCR, London, July 1993, paragraph 4.2.14. See Conclusion No. 85 (XLIX) 1998 UNHCR Executive Committee, paragraph (aa).

118 *Neue Zürcher Zeitung*, 8 April 1994, *Frankfurter Rundschau*, 11 April 1994.

119 The European Court of Human Rights has upheld the German approach; see, for example, *Haliti v. Germany*, Application No. 31182/96, decision of 3 December 1997.

is based on the assumption that there is an international principle by virtue of which a person who has left his country in order to escape persecution must apply for recognition of refugee status and/or for asylum in the first safe country he has been able to reach. Although the persistent repetition of this assumption has led many to accept it uncritically, the reality is that no such an international principle exists and that the claim which has been advanced to this effect appears to be the product of a misreading of the principle of 'first country of asylum'. As such, removals of asylum seekers to third countries carried out solely on the basis of this supposed principle risk running counter to accepted principles of refugee protection and may involve breaches of the international obligations of the removing country under the 1951 Convention."[120]

The extent to which the responsibility of the expelling state is engaged under the European Convention on Human Rights in these situations has been examined by both the Commission and the Court.

In *Amuur v. France*[121] a complaint under Article 3 was declared inadmissible by the Commission because the Somali applicants were returned to Syria, where they were not at risk and there was no evidence to suggest that Syria would have returned them to Somalia.

The Convention also forbids expulsion to states which do not have the necessary procedural guarantees to protect individuals from onward expulsion to situations where they will be at risk. The clarification of Convention law is of crucial importance in the light of the many readmission agreements which are now being concluded, both bilaterally and between the European Union and other territories, particularly in central and eastern Europe and the former Soviet Union and beyond.

In the case of *T.I. v. the United Kingdom*[122] the Court noted that, under the Convention, contracting parties' obligations do not stop at protecting people from expulsion to states where they will risk ill-treatment. The case concerned a Sri Lankan asylum seeker who had been refused asylum in Germany because he feared persecution by non-state agents and because his claim was not considered credible by the German authorities. He was being returned there by the United Kingdom under the (then) Dublin Convention. On the facts, his claim to asylum, had it been examined in the United Kingdom, would have been likely to succeed. The European Court considered that the evidence showed grave concerns that he would be at risk if returned to Sri Lanka. The Court accepted the German Government's assurances that he would be able to submit a second asylum claim. It was, however, not only conceded that he would be unlikely to succeed in this, but also that he would be unable to benefit

---

120 *The "safe third country" policy in the light of the international obligations of countries* vis-à-vis *refugees and asylum seekers*, UNHCR, London, July 1993, paragraphs 1.1 and 1.2.

121 Application No. 19776/92, judgment of 25 June 1996.

122 Application No. 43844/98, decision of 7 March 2000.

from the specific provisions of German law relating to the application of Article 3 of the European Convention on Human Rights as a basis for protection from expulsion. The German case law on Article 3 was in direct conflict with that of the ECtHR itself in that it did not at that time accord protection to those at risk from non-state agents (see above). The Court eventually accepted the German Government's assurances that there was in place another discretionary procedure which would fill the "protection gap" that would otherwise exist. The case was therefore declared inadmissible.

Some two weeks after this decision another asylum seeker was removed from the United Kingdom to Germany. Despite the assurances given to the Court in *T.I.* by the Government of Germany he was neither permitted to submit a fresh claim nor to access the discretionary procedure and was sent by the border guards onward to his own country where he was arrested and ill-treated. Concern has been expressed that the decision in *T.I.* did not meet the Convention's requirement that the rights guaranteed must be "practical and effective, not theoretical and illusory".

Within the context of the EU measures it is interesting to note that the Qualification Directive applies to many of those in need of subsidiary protection but who are not Geneva Convention refugees. However, the Dublin Convention (now Regulation) refers only to those who seek Geneva Convention refugee status. An individual who does not claim to be a Geneva Convention refugee, but expressly seeks the protection of Article 3 of the European Convention on Human Rights, can therefore presumably still not be lawfully made subject to Dublin Regulation procedures.

The test under the European Convention on Human Rights remains the same for all these cases. Is there a real risk of exposure to ill-treatment, either in the state of proposed destination or through chain *refoulement?* If there is an arguable violation, is there an effective remedy?

In some cases applicants have been expelled, but been returned by order of the national courts, like the applicants in *Vilvarajah* (whose complaint was rejected in Strasbourg and who were ill-treated on return).[123] In other cases the role of other treaty bodies can be important. In *Paez v. Sweden,*[124] two Peruvian brothers had applied for asylum in Sweden. Both were excluded from refugee status on similar grounds (under Article 1F of the Geneva Convention). One brother then made an application to the European Commission of Human Rights, the other to the United Nations Committee against Torture. The Commission found in April 1996 that the applicant would not be at risk if returned to Peru. A year later, the United Nations Committee against Torture found that the return of the applicant's brother would expose him to prohibited

---

123 See, for example, *D.S., S.N., and B.T. v. France*, Application No. 18560/91, decision of 16 October 1992, *Iruretagoyena v. France*, Application No. 32829/96, decision of 12 January 1998.

124 *Paez v. Sweden*, Application No. 29482/95, decision of 18 April 1996.

treatment and underlined the absolute nature of the protection.[125] The Swedish Government then granted a residence permit to the brother despite the fact that the application to the Strasbourg institutions had been rejected. The Court held that the case could be struck off without deciding whether or not the proposed expulsion would have been a violation of the Convention.

B.B. v. France[126] concerned the proposed expulsion to the then Zaire of an Aids sufferer whose four brothers had all been granted asylum in France or Belgium. The applicant was made subject to a compulsory residence order, but not granted a residence permit, after the Commission's report found that his expulsion would violate Article 3. The application was therefore struck off by the Court.

A significant number of cases are struck off in this way each year because, following the making of a complaint to the European Court, the government decides to withdraw the threat of expulsion. In *Abdurahim Incedursun v. the Netherlands*,[127] the Commission had found no violation of Article 2, Protocol No. 6 or Article 3 of the Convention. However, the applicants had succeeded in having their complaint referred to the Court under Protocol No. 9 of the Convention. Once the Filtering Committee had passed the application for onward reference to the Court, the Netherlands Government granted the applicant a residence permit. This mirrors the conduct of the same government in the case of *Nsona*.[128]

4. The significance of the jurisprudence of the UNCAT Committee

The jurisprudence in this field of the Committee against Torture under UNCAT is not just informative but has a legal role in the interpretation of the European Convention on Human Rights. Article 53[129] of the European Convention on Human Rights provides that a provision of the Convention may not be applied in a way that is inconsistent with the other international obligations of the state in question.[130]

---

125 Decision of 28 April 1997, Communication No. 39/1996, UN Decision CAT/C/18/D/39/1996.

126 *B.B. v. France*, Application No. 30930/96, judgment of 7 September 1998.

127 *Abdurahim Incedursun v. the Netherlands*, Application No. 33124/96, judgment of 22 June 1999.

128 *Nsona v. the Netherlands*, Application No. 23366/94, judgment of 28 November 1996. This case was not struck off because the applicant had actually been expelled and then permitted to return without the government acknowledging that the expulsion was a violation of the Convention.

129 "Nothing in this Convention shall be construed as limiting or derogating from any of the human rights and fundamental freedoms which may be ensured under the laws of any High Contracting Party or under any other agreement to which it is a party."

130 See also *Soering v. the United Kingdom*, Application No. 14038/88, judgment of 7 July 1989.

Signatories to the UNCAT are bound under Article 3 of that Convention to refrain from returning an individual to a state in which they would be exposed to acts of torture. A complaints mechanism to ensure that this prohibition is complied with exists in the form of the Committee against Torture, which has competence to hear complaints relating to a State's violation of its obligations under the treaty provisions. Whilst criticism has been levelled at the committee for the limited circumstances in which it will conclude that a state has violated the treaty, it should be noted that its decisions are necessarily restricted by the specific scope of UNCAT's provisions as outlined in greater detail below. These limitations are perhaps at fault for the narrow manner in which the jurisprudence of the committee has developed in recent years, a position which is no doubt highly frustrating, if not severely detrimental, to those applicants who remain outside the Convention's safeguards.

Article 1 of the UNCAT makes clear that torture must be inflicted by or with the acquiescence of the state. Acquiescence implies complicity. A higher level of state complicity is required than a mere reluctance or *a fortiori* inability to take sufficiently robust measures to prevent the torture occurring at the hands of non-state agents. Article 1 outlines that a violation will only be found in situations where it can be shown that a state's actions or proven acquiescence will result in an individual facing a risk of torture. As a result of the natural interpretation of this provision, the committee is unable to ensure that an individual is not deported to a country in which the feared abuse will be inflicted by a non-state actor.

An exception, however, exists with regard to "acts by groups exercising quasi-governmental authority"[131] who have de facto control over the territory to which the return of an individual is proposed. The committee has deemed that such "groups" must effectively undertake "certain prerogatives"[132] that are comparable to those traditionally associated with a legitimate government. However, the extent of this exception is somewhat limited in terms of the situations in which the committee has interpreted it to apply. Notably, as in *H.M.H.I. v. Australia*,[133] even where a centralised government maintains limited territorial control and is of a transitional nature, the committee is unlikely to consider a dominant regional faction as exercising the requisite "quasi-governmental" power to be subject to the protection afforded by the convention.

---

131 *H.M.H.I. v. Australia*, Communication No. 177/2001, UN Doc. A/57/44, p. 166 (2002), 1 May 2002.

132 *Elmi v. Australia*, Communication No. 120/1998, UN Doc. CAT/C/22/D/120/1998 (1999), 14 May 1999.

133 *H.M.H.I. v. Australia*, Communication No. 177/2001, UN Doc. A/57/44, p. 166 (2002), 1 May 2002.

Article 16 of the UNCAT specifies that certain articles of the convention also apply to inhuman and degrading treatment as well as to torture. (The different levels of treatment are equally absolutely prohibited by the ECHR.) Article 3 is not among the articles specifically mentioned in Article 16. In terms of the approach adopted when assessing a communication, a number of considerations have been regarded as instructive when examining the risk faced by an individual. The committee appears to place particular reliance on the existence of previous acts of torture,[134] the length of time that has passed since the previous abuse occurred,[135] the political profile of the author[136] and any pattern of consistent human rights violations in the receiving state.[137] The standard to be applied to the reality of the risk feared need not be "highly probable", but must be "personal, present, foreseeable, and real". These requirements impose a rather exacting standard to satisfy, a problem which is no doubt further exacerbated by the restrictive burden of proof imposed upon the individual who is required to demonstrate a prima facie case despite the committee's general unwillingness to re-examine a state's domestic factual findings.[138]

Nevertheless, a number of important principles have emerged from the decisions of the committee, particularly in relation to credibility. In *Kisoki v. Sweden*[139] it was expressly recognised that it was normal for people who have been tortured not to disclose the detailed story of their experiences fully at the time they are interviewed and that this should not damage an asylum claimant's credibility. This position was reaffirmed in *Karoui v. Sweden*,[140] where the committee noted the importance it attached to the individual's explanation for the inconsistencies in the information provided to the state party during the asylum process. However, where there is a delay in adducing documentary evidence, such as where the individual waits until after the initial decision of a state authority, the committee appears to be loath to accept these documents' authenticity without a "coherent" explanation as to why they were not produced at an earlier

134 *K.K. v. Switzerland,* Communication No. 186/2001, UN Doc. CAT/C/31/D/186/2001 (2003), 11 November 2003.

135 Ibid.

136 *S.U.A. v. Sweden,* Communication No. 223/2002, U.N. Doc. CAT/C/33/D/223/2002 (2004), 22 November 2004.

137 *Mutombo v. Switzerland,* Communication No. 13/1993, U.N. Doc. A/49/44, p. 45 (1994).

138 *P.E. v. France,* Communication No. 193/2001, U.N. Doc. CAT/C/29/D/193/2001 (2002), 21 November 2002.

139 *Kisoki v. Sweden,* Communication No. 41/1996, U.N. Doc. CAT/C/16/D/41/1996 (1996).

140 *Karoui v. Sweden,* Communication No. 185/200, U.N. Doc. A/57/44, p. 198 (2002).

stage.[141] This rationale also appears to extend to situations in which the individual has waited until the appeal stage of their request for asylum before alleging that they face a risk of torture if returned to a particular state.[142]

The committee has also made significant comments concerning a state's reliance on "diplomatic assurances" to circumvent the protection against refoulement of an individual to an abusive state. Whilst such assurances were seemingly accepted as valid in *Hanan Ahmed Fouad Abd El Khalek Attia v. Sweden*,[143] it would appear that the committee based its decision in that instance primarily on the lack of personal risk to the individual and the fact that the guarantees had been strictly monitored and upheld in the time that had passed. In contrast, the later decision in *Agiza v. Sweden*[144] clearly establishes that diplomatic assurances cannot provide sufficient protection where there is a manifest risk of torture, especially where there is no effective mechanism for the "*refouling*" state to enforce them.

Another pertinent issue that has been considered is that of the applicability of an internal flight alternative, discussed in *Alan v. Switzerland*.[145] Here an argument that an individual could simply relocate within a state's territory was dismissed on the basis that there was little likelihood that whilst an active police search existed a safe area could be found. However, the subsequent decision specifically concerning India in *S.S.S. v. Canada*[146] outlines that where an individual does not have a particularly high political profile, and a substantial period of time has passed since any police interest, the ability to locate a safe haven elsewhere in the country of origin is substantially increased.

5. The extraterritorial application of other articles of the ECHR

The Court has been primarily concerned with situations where expulsion would engage Article 3. This section looks at the other articles of the Convention which might be engaged extraterritorially.

---

141 *H.B. H., T.N. T., H.J. H., H.O. H., H.R. H. and H.G. H. v. Switzerland*, Communication No. 192/2001, 29 April 2003.

142 *H.K.H. v. Sweden*, Communication No. 204/2002, U.N. Doc. CAT/C/29/D/204/2002 (2002), 19 November 2002.

143 *Hanan Ahmed Fouad Abd El Khalek Attia v. Sweden*, Communication No. 199/2002, U.N. Doc. AT/C/31/D/199/2002 (2003), 17 November 2003.

144 *Agiza v. Sweden*, Communication No. 233/2003, U.N. Doc. CAT/C/34/D/233/2003 (2005), 20 May 2005.

145 *Alan v. Switzerland*, Communication No. 21/1995, U.N. Doc. CAT/C/16/D/21/1995 (1996).

146 *S.S.S. v. Canada*, Communication No. 245/2004, U.N. Doc. CAT/C/35/D/245/2004 (2005).

Article 2 – The right to life[147]

The Court found in *Soering*[148] that it could not be considered a breach of Article 2 read together with Article 3 to expel a person to face the death penalty since Article 2 did not outlaw capital punishment. However, for those states which are parties to Protocol No. 6 to the Convention (concerning the abolition of the death penalty), it has since been held that it can be a breach of that protocol to extradite or expel a person to another state where there is a real risk that the death penalty will be imposed.[149] The asylum seeker or refugee who would face capital charges or execution on return will thus be protected from expulsion in a state which has ratified Protocol No. 6 and, *a fortiori*, Protocol No. 13 (concerning the abolition of the death penalty in all circumstances).

The Article 2 issue has not generally been raised in expulsion cases. Although the applicant in *H.L.R. v. France*[150] alleged that his life would be at risk if he returned to Colombia, the matter was considered under Article 3. The case of *D. v. the United Kingdom*[151] was declared admissible under Article 2 but the Court preferred to examine it on the merits under Article 3, as did the Commission in *Bahaddar*.[152] The case of *M.A.R. v. the United Kingdom*[153] was also declared admissible under Article 2 where the applicant alleged he could face arbitrary execution on return to Iran.[154]

---

147 Article 2 provides:
"1. Everyone's right to life shall be protected by law. No one shall be deprived of his life intentionally save in the execution of a sentence of a court following his conviction of a crime for which this penalty is provided by law.
2. Deprivation of life shall not be regarded as inflicted in contravention of this article when it results from the use of force which is no more than absolutely necessary:
a. in defence of any person from unlawful violence;
b. in order to effect a lawful arrest or to prevent the escape of a person lawfully detained;
c. in action lawfully taken for the purpose of quelling a riot or insurrection."

148 *Soering v. the United Kingdom*, Application No. 14038/88, judgment of 7 July 1989, paragraph 103.

149 *Y v. the Netherlands*, Application No. 16531/90, 68 DR 299. *Aylor Davis v. France*, 76 DR 164. *Leong Chong v. Portugal*, Series A, No. 83A, DR 88. *Alla Raidl v. Austria*, Application No. 25342/94, decision of 4 November 1995.

150 *H.L.R. v. France*, Application No. 24573/94, judgment of 29 April 1997.

151 *D. v. the United Kingdom*, Application No. 30240/96, judgment of 2 May 1997.

152 *Bahaddar v. the Netherlands*, Application No. 25894/94, decision of 22 May 1995.

153 *M.A.R. v. the United Kingdom*, Application No. 28038/95, decision of 16 January 1997.

154 Ibid.

A comprehensive analysis of the current approach adopted by the Court when considering the extraterritorial application of Article 2 was undertaken in *Bader v. Sweden*.[155] Although it was recognised that state practice has yet to amend Article 2 so as to abolish the death penalty in all circumstances, it did acknowledge that a "deprivation of life pursuant to an 'execution of a sentence of a court'"[156] would need to comply rigorously with the standards enshrined in Article 6. Relying on the judgment in *Öcalan v. Turkey*,[157] the Court expressed the view that:

> "an issue may arise under Articles 2 and 3 of the Convention if a Contracting State deports an alien who has suffered or risks suffering a flagrant denial of a fair trial in the receiving State, the outcome of which was or is likely to be the death penalty".[158]

Under this rationale the Court in *Bader* found that a death sentence imposed following a "flagrant denial of a fair trial"[159] prohibited the respondent state from returning the applicant to Syria. In a concurring opinion, however, this finding of a violation under Article 2 was considered inappropriate by Judge Cabral Barreto,[160] who expressed the view that the state's actions would more sensibly be defined as a breach of Article 1 of Protocol No. 13.[161]

Article 1 of Protocol No. 6 – No one shall be condemned to the death penalty or executed

The Court has established that an individual may not be extradited to another country where there are substantial and proven grounds for believing that the individual will be subject to the death penalty. This is, however, as in *Al-Shari v. Italy*,[162] conditional on the individual first adducing prima facie evidence to substantiate any such risk.

In EU states, Article 15a of the Qualification Directive requires that "subsidiary protection" including protection from return is granted to those at risk of the death penalty or execution.

---

155 *Bader v. Sweden*, Application No. 13284/04, judgment of 8 November 2005.

156 Ibid., paragraph 42, referencing the Court in *Öcalan v. Turkey*, Application No. 46221/99, judgment (GC) of 12 May 2005.

157 *Öcalan v. Turkey*, see above.

158 *Bader v. Sweden*, Application No. 13284/04, judgment of 8 November 2005, paragraph 42.

159 Ibid., paragraph 47.

160 Ibid.

161 See below, Article 1 of Protocol No. 13.

162 *Al-Shari v. Italy*, Application No. 57/03, decision of 5 June 2005.

Article 1 of Protocol No. 13 – No one shall be condemned to the death penalty or executed even in times of war

Whilst the Court has yet to unanimously find a violation, the nature of this prohibition has been examined in the concurring opinion of Judge Cabral Barreto in *Bader v. Sweden*.[163] In joining the Court's majority finding of a violation of Article 2 for an applicant who faced the death penalty if deported to Syria, the concurring opinion went on to establish that such a complaint would be more appropriately categorised as breaching Article 1 of Protocol No. 13. In making this analysis, Judge Cabral Barreto placed reliance on the intention of the signatory states to the additional protocol to strengthen and replace the obligation under Article 2 so that the abolition of the death penalty applied in all circumstances.

Article 4 and Article 9 – Freedom of thought, conscience and religion, freedom from forced labour and conscientious objection

The Court has still declined to accept that the refusal of ECHR states to recognise conscientious objection to military service violates the provisions of either Article 4 or Article 9.[164] What it has instead focused on is the ancillary consequences of this refusal (see, for example, *Thlimmenos v. Greece*).[165] In *Ülke v. Turkey*, it took the position it had adopted in *Thlimmenos* further. In *Ülke* (not an expulsion case), the applicant faced indefinite repeated punishment for his refusal to serve: he had already been forced to serve eight sentences for failure to wear his military uniform, only to be brought back to his regiment after each release and arrested again. The fact that he was forced into hiding and "civil death" (and could not, for instance, marry the mother of his child), coupled with the absence of procedural safeguards, was sufficient to bring the consequences of his inability to enjoy the right to conscientious objection within the ambit of Article 3.

Article 9, paragraph 2(e), and Article 15 of the Qualification Directive[166] may bring the refusal to do military service within the scope of the directive.

---

163 *Bader v. Sweden*, Application No. 13284/04, judgment of 8 November 2005.

164 The Charter of Fundamental Rights of the European Union, proclaimed in December 2000, states specifically in Article 10, paragraph 2: "The right to conscientious objection is recognised, in accordance with the national laws governing the exercise of this right."

165 Application No. 34369/97, judgment of 6 July 2000.

166 Article 9, paragraph 2(e), defines as persecution "prosecution or punishment for refusal to perform military service in a conflict, where performing military service would include crimes or acts falling under the exclusion clauses …".

Article 5 – Liberty and security of the person

The Court has not to date delivered any judgment concerning the extraterritorial application of Article 5. In *Olaechea v. Spain*[167] the applicant's complaint included allegations that he would be subjected to arbitrary detention on extradition to Peru, but the Court's combined admissibility decision and judgment chose not to deal with this aspect of the application. In *Tomic v. the United Kingdom* the Court found that for either Article 5 or Article 6 to apply extra-territorially "the risk must be of arbitrary detention or unfair proceedings that reach the flagrant level necessary for the expulsion to raise issues under [those articles]" – mere technical imperfections will not suffice.

Article 6 – The right to a fair trial

The Court held in *Soering*:

> "[t]he right to a fair trial in criminal proceedings, as embodied in Article 6, holds a prominent place in a democratic society. The Court does not exclude that an issue might exceptionally be raised under Article 6 by an extradition decision in circumstances where the fugitive has suffered or risks suffering a flagrant denial of fair trial in the requesting country. However the facts of the present case do not disclose such a risk."[168]

In *Hilal v. the United Kingdom* the Court found admissible the complaint regarding the applicant's allegation that on expulsion he would face arbitrary and unfair criminal proceedings, but, having found a violation of Article 3, found that no separate issue arose.

In *Drozd and Janousek v. France and Spain* the Court noted that "the Convention does not require the Contracting Parties to impose its standards on third states or territories",[169] and referred to the importance of strengthening international co-operation in the administration of justice. It went on to state that "the Contracting states are, however, obliged to refuse their co-operation if it emerges that the conviction is the result of a flagrant denial of justice".[170]

This obligation must apply *a fortiori* in cases of threatened expulsion to face trial in a country which flagrantly abuses the most fundamental principles of fair trial,[171] particularly where such a trial could result in the imposition of the death penalty. See *Öcalan* and *Bader* (above).

---

167 *Olaechea Cahuas v. Spain,* Application No. 24668/03, judgment of 10 August 2006.

168 *Soering v. the United Kingdom*, Application No. 14038/88, judgment of 7 July 1989, paragraph 113.

169 Application No. 12747/87, judgment of 26 June 1992, paragraph 110.

170 Ibid.

171 See *M.A.R. v. the United Kingdom*, Application No. 28038/95, 16 January 1997; *Hilal v. the United Kingdom*, Application No. 45276/99, decision of 8 February 2000.

Finally, in the Grand Chamber judgment of *Mamatkulov and Askarov v. Turkey*[172] the Court considered the application of Article 6 to the fairness of criminal proceedings in Uzbekistan. The Court considered that, like the risk of treatment proscribed by Articles 2 and/or 3, "the risk of a flagrant denial of justice in the country of destination must primarily be assessed by reference to the facts which the Contracting State knew or should have known when it extradited the persons concerned".[173]

Although, in the light of the information available, there may have been reasons for doubting at the time that they would receive a fair trial in the state of destination, there was not sufficient evidence to show that any possible irregularities in the trial were liable to constitute a flagrant denial of justice within the meaning of paragraph 113 of *Soering*. However, had Turkey not failed to comply with the indication given by the Court under Rule 39, the Court would have benefited from having additional information to assist it in its assessment of whether or not there was a real risk of a flagrant denial of justice.

One can only speculate if a violation of Article 6, paragraph 1, would have been found in such circumstances.

As will be discussed below, Article 6 does not apply to the asylum determination process in the country where asylum is sought.

Article 7 – Freedom from retrospective criminal offences and punishment[174]

The Court found in *Gabarri Moreno v. Spain*[175] that the failure of the Spanish domestic courts to reduce the applicant's sentence in accordance with the relevant law on mitigating circumstances violated Article 7.[176] However, where the failure to reduce the sentence in accordance with the law of the sentencing state occurs extraterritorially the Court has taken a different approach. The cases of *Csoszanski v. Sweden*[177] and *Szabo v. Sweden*[178] concerned convicted

---

172 *Mamatkulov and Askarov v. Turkey*, Applications Nos. 46827/99 and 46951/99, judgment of 4 February 2005.

173 Ibid., paragraph 90.

174 Article 7 states: "No one shall be held guilty of any criminal offence on account of any act or omission which did not constitute a criminal offence under national or international law at the time when it was committed. Nor shall a heavier penalty be imposed than the one that was applicable at the time the criminal offence was committed."

175 Application No. 68066/01, judgment of 22 July 2003.

176 In the case of *Grava v. Italy*, Application No. 43522/98, judgment of 10 July 2003, in different circumstances it was held to violate Article 5, paragraph 1(a).

177 Application No. 22318/02, decision of 26 October 2006.

178 Application No. 28578/03, decision of 27 June 2006.

criminals who were transferred – involuntarily – under the Protocol to the Convention on the Transfer of Sentenced Persons to serve their sentences in a state where they would not benefit from the normal significant reduction in time actually spent in prison that would have been applied had they remained in the sentencing state. The Court found that this disclosed no violation of the Convention. The reasoning is difficult to follow. It would seem logical to apply the reasoning previously adduced in relation to Article 6 of the Convention to Article 7. The argument in favour of this approach is strengthened by the fact that – like Articles 2, 3, and 4, paragraph 1, but unlike Article 6 – Article 7 cannot be derogated from even in time of war or national emergency.[179] The sentencing judge in the sentencing state, being familiar with domestic law and practice, knows exactly how much time the convicted individual is likely to spend in custody and the – often purely notional – length of the sentence imposed reflects this reality. It is difficult to see how an unanticipated non-voluntary return to face a significantly longer period of incarceration than that anticipated by the sentencing judge is compatible with the spirit if not the letter of Article 7.

Article 4 of Protocol No. 7 – Prohibition on double jeopardy

Issues relating to the prohibition on double jeopardy can arise in the context of the risk of people being prosecuted again on return to their home state for the offence of which they have already been convicted and for which they have already served a sentence in the expelling state. However, Article 4 of Protocol No. 7 only applies to repeated prosecution in the same state and not in different states. In the case of *Amrollahi v. Denmark* the Court declared inadmissible a case where an individual alleged that prosecution for the crime for which he had already been punished would await him if expelled.

The situation of an expulsion order that is imposed in addition to an ordinary penal sanction for a criminal conviction as an Article 4, Protocol No. 7, issue is discussed below at page 73.

Article 8 – The right to physical and moral integrity

This article may be engaged in two ways in the context of asylum and of expulsion or exclusion from the territory. The right to moral and physical integrity as an important aspect of private life will be considered here, and the right to respect for family life will be considered below at page 95 *et seq.*

The Convention organs have been keenly aware of the absolute nature of Article 3. It is illimitable: no limitation can be put on its application. It is unjustifiable: no argument can be advanced to exculpate the offending state. It is non-derogable: it is binding even in time of war or national emergency. Thus

---

179 The decision in *X v. the Netherlands*, Application No. 7512/76, 6 DR 184 (1974), should be read in the light of the cumulative later general Convention jurisprudence.

a stringent test is applied to all forms of treatment in order that the fundamental importance of Article 3 and the absolute nature of the right are maintained.

However, the Court has recognised that actual or threatened treatment which does not reach the high "threshold of severity" test under Article 3 is nevertheless unacceptable in a democratic society. The Court has consequently developed the notion that where there are sufficiently adverse effects on a person's "physical and moral integrity", this may breach Article 8 in its private life aspect. In *Costello-Roberts v. the United Kingdom*[180] the Court considered that physical and psychological ill-treatment which fell below the threshold of Article 3 might nevertheless be in breach of Article 8.

There is no exhaustive definition of the term "private life" and Article 8 protects broad elements of the personal sphere, such as "gender identification, name and sexual orientation and sexual life".[181] In addition, mental health is a vital aspect of the right to private life associated with the aspect of moral and physical integrity. The preservation of mental stability is indispensable to the effective enjoyment of the right to respect for private life since Article 8 protects a "right to identity and personal development, and the right to establish and develop relationships with other human beings in the outside world".[182] In expulsion cases, where deportation cannot be prevented on the grounds that the applicant will be subjected to mental suffering or deterioration falling short of inhuman or degrading treatment under Article 3, it may fall within the scope of Article 8. In *D. v. the United Kingdom*,[183] the Court declined to consider the complaints under Article 8 as it found that the expulsion would amount to a violation of Article 3. The same was true in the case of *Hilal v. the United Kingdom*.[184]

The applicant in *Bensaid v. the United Kingdom*[185] was a schizophrenic suffering from a psychotic illness therefore posing a risk of harm to others, and to himself. Despite a doctor's report stating that the implementation of a decision to deport

---

180 Application No. 13134/87, judgment of 25 March 1993, pp. 60-61, paragraph 36.

181 *Bensaid v. the United Kingdom*, Application No. 44599/98, judgment of 6 February 2001. See, for example, *Dudgeon v. the United Kingdom*, Application No. 7525/76, judgment of 22 October 1981, paragraph 41; *B. v. France*, Application No. 13343/87, judgment of 25 March 1992, paragraph 63; *Burghartz v. Switzerland*, Application No. 16213/90, decision of 22 February 1994, paragraph 24; and *Laskey, Jaggard and Brown v. the United Kingdom*, Applications Nos. 21627/93, 21826/93 and 21974/93, judgment of 19 February 1997, paragraph 36.

182 *Bensaid v. the United Kingdom*, p. 47, citing *Burghartz v. Switzerland*, cited above, and *Friedl v. Austria*, Application No. 15225/89, judgment of 31 January 1995. Followed in *Paramsothy v. the Netherlands*, Application No. 14492/03, decision of 10 November 2005.

183 *D. v. the United Kingdom*, Application No. 30240/96, judgment of 2 May 1997.

184 *Hilal v. the United Kingdom*, Application No. 45276/99, judgment of 6 March 2001.

185 Op. cit.

the applicant to Algeria would result in a deterioration in his mental health, the Court held that it had not been established that the applicant's moral integrity would be "substantially affected to a degree falling within the scope of Article 8".[186] The case of *Paramsothy v. the Netherlands* was declared inadmissible on a similar basis.[187]

What, then, must the applicant show to establish that a future deterioration in their physical or mental health, as a result of the implementation of an expulsion decision, meets the threshold of Article 8? *Bensaid* established that the risk of deterioration in mental health must not be speculative or hypothetical to meet the test under Article 3, but must be "substantially affected"[188] for the purposes of Article 8. Whilst there is rigorous scrutiny of the existence of ill-treatment alleged to breach Article 3,[189] the degree of documentation or substantiation necessary for a claim to succeed under either Article 3 or 8 seems unclear – particularly in relation to expulsion cases concerning a person's psychological or mental integrity. The Court has considered that it might be unreasonable for a mentally disturbed person to give a "detailed or coherent description" of the suffering which has been inflicted.[190] For example, in *Bensaid* and *Paramsothy*, medical evidence and doctors' reports were adduced as to the serious risk posed to the applicants' mental health if a deportation decision was implemented. The jurisprudence suggests that even if the Court accepts the seriousness of a medical condition, a claim may still be held to be unsubstantiated.[191] However, in *F. v. the United Kingdom*,[192] the Court held that whilst in *Dudgeon*[193] a ban on homosexuality could give rise to an interference with a person's moral and physical integrity, in the context of asylum, and on a "purely pragmatic basis, it cannot be required that an expelling state only returns an alien to a country which is in full and effective enforcement" of all the Convention rights. This represents a hard line on this aspect of the extraterritorial application of Article 8 (and presumably other Convention rights which are not regarded as those fundamental in a democratic society, such as Articles 2 and 3 (and 4)).

The threshold of the severity test is not the sole distinction between the protection guaranteed by Article 8 and Article 3. As seen above, once treatment

---

186 Ibid., paragraph 48.

187 *Paramsothy v. the Netherlands*, Application No. 14492/03, decision of 10 November 2005.

188 *Bensaid v. the United Kingdom*, op. cit., paragraph 3.

189 See, for example, *Vilvarajah and Others v. United Kingdom*, Applications Nos. 13163/87, 13164/87, 13165/87, 13447/87 and 13448/87, judgment of 30 October 1991.

190 *Aerts v. Belgium*, Application No. 25357/94, judgment of 30 July 1998.

191 *Ovdienko v. Switzerland*, Application No. 1383/04, decision of 31 May 2005.

192 *F. v. the United Kingdom*, Application No. 36812/02, decision of 31 August 2004.

193 *Dudgeon v. the United Kingdom*, Application No. 7525/76, judgment of 22 October 1981.

is established to fall within Article 3, the absolute nature of the right means that the level of protection afforded cannot be reduced. In contrast, an interference with Article 8 rights can be justified under the second paragraph subject to the respondent government successfully establishing that the interference was carried out in accordance with the law, pursued a legitimate aim and was proportionate to the aim pursued. These tests will be considered below in the context of "family" and "private life". The Court did not engage in a proportionality test in the above cases, no violation having been found. However, in the *Bensaid* and *Paramsothy* cases the Court held that even if an interference could be found with Article 8 in its "private life" aspect, it would be an interference carried out pursuant to the legitimate aim of the "economic well-being of the country", as is frequently and broadly the case in many asylum cases.

6. Procedural guarantees and the right to an effective remedy where expulsion is threatened

The rights guaranteed under the Convention and set out above depend on the buttressing of procedural guarantees if they are to be practical and effective, not theoretical and illusory, as the Convention requires.[194]

In some cases the absence of procedural safeguards in the expelling country will play an important role in the Court's assessment. *Hassanpour-Omrani v. Sweden*[195] and *Jabari v. Turkey*[196] both concerned women who feared stoning on return to Iran because of adultery. The Swedish case was declared inadmissible by the Commission. In contrast the Turkish case, where there were no procedural safeguards, was declared admissible by the Court.

Access to asylum determination procedures

Since the mid-1980s western European states have consistently tightened regulations and procedures in order to reduce the incentives for asylum seekers to come to western Europe and thus to reduce the number of claims they are required to process in what are known as "mixed flows" as well as to save having to weed out those whose asylum claims are "manifestly unfounded". In particular, states have sought to stop individuals with such claims from reaching the country and gaining access to the full asylum procedure.

Visa requirements began to be introduced from the mid-1980s for individuals coming from areas of conflict. Asylum seekers coming from safe countries of origin or via "safe third states" were also "fast tracked" and denied access to full asylum procedures. The concept of liability of carriers for transporting

---

194 *Artico v. Italy*, Application No. 6694/74, judgment of 13 May 1980.

195 *Hassanpour-Omrani v. Sweden*, Application No. 36863/97, decision of 19 October 1998.

196 *Jabari v. Turkey*, Application No. 40035/98, decision of 28 October 1999.

those without valid papers has been applied with increased rigour and the payment of fines has been imposed, in addition to the obligation on the airline to bear the cost of returning such passengers to their country of departure (see pages 63 *et seq.* below).

Western European states have also introduced accelerated asylum procedures for those with "manifestly unfounded" claims and sought to speed up procedures so that the long period spent waiting for a claim to be determined does not act as an incentive for those asylum seekers who are viewed as economic migrants and whose claims will eventually be rejected. Fingerprinting and photographing of asylum seekers are also widely used to discourage multiple and fraudulent asylum applications.[197] The Schengen signatories have set up mechanisms to avoid having to consider applications from asylum seekers whose applications have been rejected in another state.[198]

Visas

At national level, visa restrictions have the effect of limiting asylum seekers' access to the countries which impose them. The Commission found many years ago in *X v. the Federal Republic of Germany* that, in principle, the acts of visa officials in an embassy can engage the responsibility of the state concerned.[199] Later the Court in *Loizidou v. Turkey* (Preliminary Objections)[200] upheld the view which it had adopted in *Drozd and Janousek v. France and Spain*[201] that the responsibility of contracting parties can be engaged by the acts of their authorities whether performed within or outside national boundaries. This is so even if they also produce effects outside their own territory. Several cases before the Convention organs have concerned the refusal of visas to family members.[202] In most jurisdictions it is not possible to be granted a visa as an asylum seeker, and for reasons of alienage (see page 21 *et seq.* above) it is not possible to be recognised as a Geneva Convention refugee unless one is outside one's own country. In principle the Convention applies to an asylum seeker who seeks a visa from an embassy in order to flee to that embassy's country. In practice, because most diplomatic posts employ local staff in their visa sections, disclosing the basis of an asylum application before the applicant is securely outside the territory is fraught with danger. The fees charged for issuing visas are often prohibitive. For instance, when a group of Iraqi doctors, who were being forced by Saddam Hussein's regime to carry out

---

197 See, for example, Eurodac Convention.

198 Cf. Eurodac.

199 Application No. 1611/62, *Yearbook* 8 (1965), p. 158 (163).

200 Application No. 15318/89, judgment of 23 March 1995.

201 Application No. 12747/87, judgment of 26 June 1992.

202 See, for example, *Abdulaziz, Cabales and Balkandali v. the United Kingdom*, Applications Nos. 9214/80, 9473/81 and 9474/81, judgment of 28 May 1985.

punitive amputations on opponents of his regime, wanted to seek visas to escape to western Europe – but could not afford the visa fees that were being charged.

Visa requirements are used extensively by western European states, which in many instances now also require visas for passengers in transit. The ECHR institutions have always held that states are accountable before the Court *ratione loci* for decisions about visas which impinge on Convention-protected rights even when they are taken at their overseas posts. This is a classic exercise of extraterritorial jurisdiction.[203]

Carriers' liability

The enforcement of carriers' liability has also been used to limit the access of asylum seekers. Carriers' liability imposes on the airline (or less frequently, the ferry operator) responsibility for transporting someone who arrived without valid papers to another state. The airline is expected to bear the cost of returning refused passengers to their country of departure and generally also faces a fine. In the United States carriers have been fined for bringing in aliens without valid papers since the 1950s, but in Europe it is only since the late 1980s that this practice has been introduced. Earlier it was generally considered sufficient to oblige the carrier to bear the costs of returning illegal aliens. Fines were imposed from 1987 in Belgium, Germany and the United Kingdom and in Denmark from 1989, since when most of Europe has followed suit. Indeed they have been obligatory for EU member states.[204]

Legislation on carriers' liability has differed widely from state to state and has been implemented with varying degrees of thoroughness. The situation has been summed up by the Parliamentary Assembly of the Council of Europe, as follows:

> "Some countries have imposed airline sanctions which undermine the basic principles of refugee protection and the right of refugees to claim asylum while placing a considerable legal, administrative and financial burden upon carriers, and moving the responsibility away from the immigration officers."[205]

The European Court has not yet ruled on the application of visa regimes or carriers sanctions in asylum-related cases.

---

203 See, for example, *X v. Germany*, Application No. 1611/62, Court decision of 25 September 1965, *W.M. v. Denmark*, Application No. 17392/90, Commission decision of 14 October 1992, *Amekrane v. the United Kingdom*, Application No. 5961/72, Commission decision of 11 October 1973.

204 See Directive supplementing the Convention implementing the Schengen Agreement regarding financial penalties on carriers transporting third country nationals without correct documentation, 2001/51/EC, which came into force in August 2001 and required implementation by February 2003.

205 Recommendation 1163 (1991) of the Parliament Assembly of the Council of Europe on the arrival of asylum seekers at European airports, 43rd Ordinary Session, 1991, paragraph 10.

Interception on the high seas and search and rescue operations

Some individual European states, and now also the EU, have attempted to deflect the arrival of asylum seekers at their shores by intercepting the vessels in which they are travelling on the high seas. The case of *Xhavara v. Italy and Albania*[206] concerned the interception by an Italian warship of an Albanian boat which resulted in the capsize of the boat and the deaths of several of those on board. Since criminal proceedings, to which the applicants had been joined as civil parties, were still in progress in Italy the cases were rejected for failure to exhaust domestic remedies. However, the Court adopted a number of important views. It found first that Italy was accountable before the Court for the acts of its warships on the high seas; that Albania could not be held accountable by virtue of simply having signed the agreement with Italy which led to the impugned actions of the Italian warship; and, finally, that there was no issue under Article 2 of Protocol No. 4 (the right to leave) since the Albanians were not being prevented from leaving Albania, but only from reaching Italy.

Proposals are currently being discussed at EU level[207] to deal with the "mixed flows of economic migrants and asylum seekers in need of international protection leaving the north, north east and west coasts of Africa and crossing the Mediterranean".

The United Nations Convention on the Law of the Sea (UNCLOS) obliges every state to require the master of a ship which flies its flag to render assistance to any person found at sea in danger of being lost and to proceed to the rescue of persons in distress. This convention provides the framework, but the detailed obligations are found in the International Maritime Organisation (IMO) conventions. On 1 July 2006 amendments to two IMO conventions – the Safety of Life at Sea (SOLAS) and Search and Rescue (SAR) conventions entered into force which provide enhanced protection for asylum seekers and other migrants in distress.[208] The amendments are intended to ensure that the ambiguities which previously surrounded the obligations of all concerned towards those who become involved in an accident at sea are clarified. States are under an obligation to "cooperate and coordinate" to ensure that shipmasters are permitted to deliver individuals to a "place of safety", irrespective of their nationality or status. States are normally only responsible for the actions of state vessels (such as the Italian warship in the *Xhavara* case) but the obligation now extends to all masters of ships flying their flags. The duty to consider a claim for international protection exists regardless of whether the state agent in question is an embassy official, a border guard or an officer on a patrol vessel who is notified that such protection is sought.

---

206 Application No. 39473/98, decision of 11 January 2001.

207 Communication of the Commission to the Council reinforcing the management of the European Union's southern maritime borders, COM(2006)733 final, 1 December 2006.

208 See www.unhcr.org/publ/PUBL/450037d34.pdf.

Whether or not the "place of safety" referred to in the conventions can be interpreted so as to preclude landing those rescued at a port where they claim they would be exposed to a real risk of treatment prohibited under, for example, Articles 2 or 3 of the ECHR, or merely refers to safety from the threat of shipwreck and drowning, has not yet been explored by the European Convention organs.

In the Lampedusa cases[209] the applicants were rescued or intercepted at sea by the Italian authorities and taken to the Italian island of Lampedusa, from where they were returned to Libya without having the possibility to make and have considered applications for asylum.

Issues relating to the interface between the ECHR and law of the sea are likely to figure more significantly in the case law of the Court in future.

On arrival at the port or airport

Individuals arriving at ports and airports whom the authorities wish to be able to return swiftly are often kept in the transit zones of airports. It has sometimes been argued by governments that since these people have not technically entered the country they do not fall under Article 1 of the Convention as they are still in the "international zone". The Court in *Amuur* made it clear that no such concept existed in respect of the interpretation of the term of jurisdiction under Article 1 of the Convention,[210] and that the responsibilities of the state in relation to expulsion under Article 3 are engaged wherever the action of the state occurs. In *D. v. the United Kingdom* the Court noted: "Regardless of whether he ever entered the United Kingdom in the technical sense it is to be noted that he has been physically present there and thus within the jurisdiction within the meaning of Article 1. It is for the respondent state to secure to the applicant the rights guaranteed under Article 3."[211] The Lampedusa cases referred to above also raise issues of a failure to ensure access to the asylum procedure.

Issues relating to the expulsion procedure and decisions to expel

While positive obligations are placed on the national authorities in relation to the processing of asylum claims and treatment of asylum seekers, there also exists an obligation on the asylum seeker to provide, as far as possible, sufficient evidence to support their claims. In the cases of *Al-Shari and Others v. Italy*[212] and *Mogos v. Romania*,[213] the Court considered that the applicants had failed to provide specific information or adduce sufficient proof that would have enabled the Court to find a violation.

---

209 Cases *Hussun and Others v. Italy,* Application No. 10171/05, decision of 11 May 2006.

210 Application No. 19776/92, judgment of 25 June 1996. This is the only logical approach. Someone who committed a crime in the transit area of an airport would be liable to prosecution under the laws of that land.

211 Application No. 30240/96, judgment of 2 May 1997, paragraph 48.

212 *Al-Shari and Others v. Italy*, Application No. 57/03, decision of 5 June 2005.

213 *Mogos v. Romania*, Application No. 20420/02, judgment of 13 October 2005.

In *Čonka and Others v. Belgium*[214] considerable administrative and practical barriers hindered the Slovakian applicants' ability to pursue their asylum claims. The Court concluded that there had been a violation of Article 4 of Protocol No. 4.

The Court has stated on more than one occasion that national procedures must ensure that "an independent and rigorous scrutiny" is conducted on an individual's claim that his or her deportation to a third country will expose that individual to treatment prohibited by Article 3.[215] In *Jabari v. Turkey* the applicant had failed to lodge her application for asylum to the authorities within the five day requirement, as laid down in national law, and this had denied her any scrutiny of the factual basis of her fears about being removed to Iran. The Court held that such a short time limit was incompatible with the Convention.[216]

First, as explained above, the general application of the "safe third country" concept can result in an individual being successively deported to his or her country of origin where he or she might face inhuman or degrading treatment, with the result that the first deporting state might ultimately be in breach both of Article 3 of the European Convention on Human Rights and Article 33, paragraph 1, of the Geneva Convention. The use of the "safe country of origin" concept carries similar risks.

Second, the European Commission of Human Rights has clearly ruled in the cases of both *Harabi* and *Giama*[217] that the repeated "bouncing back" (or "shuttlecocking") of asylum seekers is in contravention of Article 3 of the European Convention on Human Rights.

Third, it would appear that there is a danger that the increased use of fast track procedures, against which there is often no appeal or such an appeal has no suspensive effect on the removal order, could be found to deny an asylum seeker access to an independent and impartial body capable of reviewing a decision to return him or her to a country in which he or she claims that he or she will be persecuted.

The EU has adopted a directive which sets out minimum guarantees for asylum procedures[218] which has to be transposed into national legislation in EU states by 1 December 2007.

---

214 Application No. 51564/99, judgment of 5 February 2002.

215 *Jabari v. Turkey*, Application No. 40035/98, judgment of 11 July 2000, paragraph 39.

216 Ibid., paragraph 40.

217 *Harabi v. the Netherlands*, Application No. 10798/84, decision of 5 March 1986, p. 112 (116), and *Giama v. Belgium*, DR 21, p. 73 (84).

218 Directive 2005/85.

Right to appeal or review and Article 13

Article 13 of the European Convention on Human Rights provides:

> "Everyone whose rights and freedoms as set forth in this Convention are violated shall have an effective remedy before a national authority notwithstanding that the violation has been committed by persons acting in an official capacity."

The Court decided in *Maaouia*,[219] and reaffirmed in the decision in *Mamatkulov* (see page 57 above), however, that Article 6 is not applicable to asylum and immigration proceedings. Article 13 is the only provision which can be used to strengthen the safeguards of the asylum determination process. It allows for the quality of the asylum determination procedure to be scrutinised. The respondent government in *Ramzy*[220] (pending before the European Court at the time of writing) argues that Article 13 only applies to the asylum determination process – which engages his Article 3 rights – and not to any decision to declare the applicant an undesirable alien which the Netherlands Government claims does not engage any right which the applicant claims is being violated. Since the decision that the applicant was an undesirable alien was an essential prerequisite to the decision to return him to face a situation where he claimed his Article 3 rights would be violated, it may be artificial to make a distinction of this kind between the two sets of proceedings. The judgment of the Court on this, as on the many other issues in *Ramzy*, is awaited.

The need for an arguable claim

Article 13 requires that an individual should have a remedy before a national authority in order to have his or her claim decided and, if appropriate, to obtain redress.[221] Article 13 has been consistently interpreted by the Court as requiring a remedy in domestic law only in respect of grievances which can be regarded as "arguable" in terms of the Convention.[222]

An individual only needs an arguable claim that he or she is at risk for the protection of Article 13 to be engaged. While there is no definition of "arguable", the Court in the case of *Powell and Rayner v. the United Kingdom*[223] held that a grievance could not be called unarguable even if it had been eventually

---

219 *Maaouia v. France*, Application No. 39652/98, decision of 12 January 1999.

220 *Ramzy v. the Netherlands*, Application No. 25424/05 (adjoined with *A. v. the Netherlands*, Application No. 4900/06).

221 *Klass v. Germany*, Application No. 5029/71, judgment of 6 September 1978, paragraph 64.

222 *Boyle and Rice v. the United Kingdom*, Applications Nos. 9659/82 and 9658/82, judgment of 27 April 1988.

223 Application No. 9310/81, judgment of 21 February 1990.

adjudged by the Convention organs to be "manifestly ill-founded". The Court recognised that "manifestly ill-founded" was a term of art "which extends further than the literal meaning of the word manifest would suggest at first reading".[224] It recognised that some "serious claims" might ultimately be rejected as manifestly ill-founded despite their arguable character.

It follows that under the Convention an asylum claimant who has an arguable case must have access to both asylum (or other protection) determination procedures and a national remedy in the case of refusal and the consequent threatened expulsion. The fact that the claim may later be found to be "manifestly ill-founded" in European Convention on Human Rights terms is not sufficient to excuse contracting parties from satisfying this obligation. As the Court noted in *Powell and Rayner*, the concept of "manifestly ill-founded" in Strasbourg terms is a broad one. Although the expression "manifestly unfounded" is used in various European domestic legal systems, its meaning is not necessarily the same as "manifestly ill-founded" in the European Convention on Human Rights.

Effective remedies and the (limited) extent of domestic courts' powers

Whether or not an available remedy against a refusal of asylum is effective was considered in the case of *Vilvarajah*.[225] In that case the refused asylum seekers had no right of appeal on the merits before they were sent back to Sri Lanka. The only available remedy was the administrative one of judicial review. This remedy only permits the United Kingdom courts to examine the legality of a decision and not the merits. The European Court, overturning the Commission's findings in the same case, was, however, satisfied that the way in which judicial review had operated in the applicants' case had permitted the United Kingdom courts to subject the decision to the "most anxious scrutiny".[226] It was therefore an effective remedy. Two judges (both familiar with the operation of the common law) dissented, holding that a remedy which could not examine the merits could not be described as effective.

In *Salah Sheekh* the Court found that the remedies which existed in Dutch administrative and judicial procedure were adequate because they were capable of providing the necessary remedy even though they had failed to do so in the applicant's case.

In *Chahal*, however, the Court found that the judicial review was inadequate because of the restrictions which applied in national security cases. This was because in cases where national security issues were involved, the domestic

---

224 Ibid., paragraph 32.

225 Applications Nos. 13163/87, 13164/87 and 13165/87, judgment of 30 October 1991.

226 Ibid., paragraph 125.

courts, including the ones reviewing the negative asylum decision, did not have access to the information on which the governmental authorities based their decision to expel. Therefore, they had a limited power of review.[227]

In *Jabari v.Turkey* the Court considered the procedure for determining refugee status in Turkey. The applicant's asylum request was declared inadmissible because it was lodged outside the five day deadline for such applications imposed under Turkish law. Consequently, the Turkish authorities issued an expulsion order. Despite the applicant having been granted refugee status by the UNHCR, her appeal against the deportation order before the Ankara Administrative Court was dismissed. In her application to the Court, the applicant argued that she did not have an effective remedy against the refusal to consider the asylum application and against the deportation order, since the appeal procedure did not have suspensive effect. The Court considered that "there was no assessment made by the domestic authorities of the applicant's claim to be at risk if removed to Iran".[228]

It concluded that:

> "given the irreversible nature of the harm that might occur if the risk of torture or ill-treatment alleged materialised and the importance which attaches to Article 3, the notion of an effective remedy under Article 13 requires independent and rigorous scrutiny of a claim that there exist substantial grounds for fearing a real risk of treatment contrary to Article 3 and the possibility of suspending the implementation of the measure impugned. Since the Ankara Administrative court failed in the circumstances to provide any of these safeguards, the Court is led to conclude that the judicial review proceedings relied on by the Government did not satisfy the requirements of Article 13".[229]

In line with this reasoning, the Court in *Čonka v. Belgium*[230] has further declared that "suspensive effect" must follow automatically from an application alleging a potential violation of a Convention right rather than resting solely on the discretion of the domestic authority considering the individual's case.

Čonka v. Belgium also found a violation of Article 13 taken together with Article 4 of Protocol No. 4 (the collective expulsion of aliens) because "ultimately, the alien has no guarantee ... that the Conseil d'État would deliver its decision, or even hear the case, before its expulsion, or that the authorities would allow a minimum reasonable period of grace".[231]

---

227 *Chahal v. the United Kingdom*, Application No. 22414/93, paragraphs 145, 151 and 153.

228 *Jabari v.Turkey,* op. cit., paragraph 49.

229 Ibid., paragraph 50.

230 *Čonka v. Belgium*, Application No. 51564/99, judgment of 5 February 2002.

231 *Ibid.*, paragraph 83.

Time restrictions

On the issue of the time limit of five days in which the applicant had to lodge her asylum application in *Jabari*, the Court took the view that

> "the automatic and mechanical application of such short time-limit for submitting an asylum application must be considered at variance with the protection of the fundamental value embodied in Article 3 of the Convention".[232]

The failure of a single domestic remedy to satisfy the requirements of Article 13

In situations where a single legal avenue is unable to provide an effective remedy for a violation of a Convention right, the Court may nevertheless consider that the "aggregate of several remedies"[233] provided by domestic law satisfies the requirements of Article 13. However, as demonstrated in *Kudla v. Poland*,[234] a simple assertion by the state that the individual could have raised their complaint before a number of different authorities will not suffice. Instead, the onus rests with the state to show that an "aggregate" of remedies would provide the individual with the effective relief, either compensatory or preventative, that is otherwise lacking under a single remedy.[235]

The definition of "national authority" and the right to appeal

At national level, recent legislation introduced in western European states has tended to reduce rights of appeal against a rejection of an asylum claim. Such measures have been seen not least as a way of dealing with an increase in the number of asylum applications (even though these have now been much reduced), but also to speeding up what can otherwise amount to a lengthy and cumbersome process.

As the *Golder* and *Klass*[236] cases have shown, the right set out in Article 13 of the European Convention on Human Rights to "an effective remedy before a national authority" for those "whose rights and freedoms as set forth in this Convention are violated" does not necessarily have in all instances to be a judicial authority in the strict sense.[237] However, the Court established in

---

232 Paragraph 40.

233 *Kudla v. Poland*, Application No. 30210/96, judgment of 26 October 2000, paragraph 157.

234 Ibid.

235 Ibid., paragraph 159.

236 *Golder v. the United Kingdom*, Application No. 4451/70, judgment of 21 February 1975, and *Klass v. Germany*, Application No. 5029/71, judgment of 6 September 1978.

237 European Court of Human Rights, Series A, No. 18 (1975), paragraph 33, and European Court of Human Rights, Series A, No. 28 (1978).

Conka that for a non-judicial "national authority" to satisfy the requirements of Article 13, the extent of its powers and guarantees will first be relevant in determining whether it is capable of providing an effective remedy.[238]

Legal aid

In *Richard Lee Goldstein v. Sweden*[239] the Court found that Article 13 does not guarantee a right to legal counsel paid by the state when availing oneself of such a remedy. In the Court's opinion, the absence of free legal aid in this particular case did not prevent the applicant from using the remedies at his disposal in Sweden. It could be that it is only when the absence of free legal aid directly prevents the use of the available remedies that the Court would consider Article 13 violated.

To sum up, in order to be considered as an effective remedy the procedure for granting or withholding international protection should meet a number of criteria. It should allow the competent first and second instance bodies to consider the merits of an asylum claim, it should provide the possibility of suspending any deportation order which may be in force, and it should not be constrained by a restrictive time limit within which the application must be lodged. The procedural principles emerging from the Court's jurisprudence and its interpretation of Article 13 could eventually be used in order to tackle other problems relating to asylum procedures, such as issues of excessive length of procedure or accelerated procedures. Article 13 could therefore be instrumental in establishing or assessing minimum standards applicable to asylum procedures.

The application of Article 6 – The right to a fair trial

The Court, and the Commission before it, have been invited on innumerable occasions to find that the proceedings for the determination of an asylum application, or for the review of a refusal to grant asylum, or to accede to a request to quash a decision to expel, have failed to comply with the standards of fairness set out in Article 6. The Grand Chamber has now twice made it clear that Article 6 does not apply to expulsion cases. This is because decisions regarding the entry, stay and deportation of aliens do not concern the determination of an applicant's civil rights or obligations or of a criminal charge against him, within the meaning of Article 6, paragraph 1. Rather it has been seen as an act of public authorities governed by public law.

The Grand Chamber declared admissible the case of *Maaouia v. France*,[240] which concerned the application of Article 6 to deportation and exclusion orders

---

238 *Čonka v. Belgium*, Application No. 51564/99, judgment of 5 February 2002, paragraph 75.

239 *Richard Lee Goldstein v. Sweden*, Application No. 46636/99, decision of 12 September 2000.

240 *Maaouia v. France*, Application No. 39652/98, decision of 12 January 1999.

connected to criminal proceedings. The Grand Chamber finally considered that by adopting Article 1 of Protocol No. 7 containing guarantees specifically concerning proceedings for the expulsion of aliens, the states had clearly intimated their intention not to include such proceedings within the scope of Article 6, paragraph 1, of the Convention.

The Grand Chamber has reaffirmed that position in the case of *Mamatkulov.*

Article 4 of Protocol No. 4 – Prohibition on the collective expulsion of aliens[241]

The Commission found in *Becker v. Denmark*[242] that the phrase "collective expulsion" refers to "any measure of the competent authority compelling aliens as a group to leave the country, except where such measure is taken after and on the basis of a reasonable and objective examination of the particular cases of each individual alien in the group".[243] In *Alibaks and Others v. the Netherlands,*[244] the Commission found that the fact that a number of aliens from the same country had all been refused asylum in similar terms did not mean that they had been collectively expelled when there was evidence that their cases had been individually examined.

In *Čonka v. Belgium,*[245] the Court's first ever ruling case involving the collective expulsion of Roma, the Court found that "the procedure followed [by the state authorities] did not enable it to eliminate all doubt that the expulsion might have been collective"[246] and thus decided that there was a violation of Article 4 of Protocol No. 4. The reasoning of the Court appeared to break new grounds in terms of burden of proof issues: a prima facie case under Article 4 of Protocol No. 4 would shift the burden to the government to prove that a violation has not taken place. Further, after reiterating its case law, the Court specified the definition of collective expulsion and highlighted that even where the measure was taken on the basis of a reasonable and objective examination of the particular case of each individual alien of the group,

> "that did not mean, however, that ... the background to the execution of the expulsion orders plays no further role in determining whether there has been compliance with Article 4 of Protocol No. 4".[247]

---

241 Article 4 of Protocol No. 4 states: "Collective expulsion of aliens is prohibited." (Not all member states of the Council of Europe are parties to Protocol No. 4.)

242 Application No. 7011/75, decision of 3 October 1975.

243 Ibid., p. 235.

244 Application No. 14209/88, decision of 16 December 1988.

245 *Čonka v. Belgium,* Application No. 51564/99, judgment of 5 February 2002.

246 Ibid., paragraph 63.

247 Ibid., paragraph 59.

A similar case where the Italian Government claimed to have a different intention from that of the Belgian Government in the *Čonka* case, namely to improve the living conditions of legal immigrants,[248] was struck out of the list after reaching a settlement without the Court having the opportunity to confirm the *Čonka* judgment's orientation.

In May 2006 the Court declared admissible under this provision four complaints brought against Italy by a total of almost one hundred applicants who alleged that they had been expelled collectively from Lampedusa (an Italian island near the coast of Africa) to Libya.[249] Judgment is awaited.

The application of Article 4 of Protocol No. 7 to expulsion imposed as an additional penalty

Foreigners who are convicted of criminal offences are frequently subjected to expulsion measures in addition to the criminal sanction imposed on them.

In *Üner v. the Netherlands*[250] the Court emphasised that such "administrative" measures were designed essentially to protect the interests of society and as such were preventative rather than punitive in nature. This was deemed to be the case even where a non-national could show a strong residence status and a high degree of integration within the state.[251] Criticism of this stance was, however, expressed in the joint dissenting opinion of Judges Costa, Zupančič and Türman, who reasoned that the simple dismissal of expulsion as preventative rather than punitive wholly ignored the view that these measures often "shatter"[252] lives and can constitute "as severe a penalty as a term of imprisonment, if not more severe".[253]

7. Forced expulsion of reluctant deportees

Article 3 (and the moral and physical integrity dimension of Article 8) apply not only to the situation which awaits the expelled individual in the receiving country, but also the manner in which the expelling state carries out the expulsion. Amnesty International has documented a significant increase in the instances of life-threatening and sometimes fatal methods of restraint states have used to carry out forced expulsions. The European Committee for the Prevention

---

248 *Sulejmanovic and Sultanovic v. Italy*, Application No. 57574/00, decision of 14 March 2002 (judgment struck out of the list on 8 November 2002).

249 *Hussun and Others v. Italy*, Applications Nos. 10171/05, 10601/05, 11593/05, and, 17165/05.

250 *Üner v. the Netherlands*, Application No. 46410/99, judgment of 18 October 2006.

251 Ibid., paragraph 56.

252 Ibid., paragraph 17 of the joint dissenting opinion of Judges Costa, Zupančič and Türman.

253 Ibid.

of Torture (CPT) – established to complement the right of petition under the ECHR and to strengthen the protection against torture or inhuman and degrading treatment – has documented the treatment of those being expelled. In addition to monitoring the procedure followed during boarding onto aeroplanes and during the flight itself, the CPT has also investigated "the detention prior to deportation, the steps taken to prepare for the immigration detainee's return to the country of destination, measures to ensure suitable selection and training of escort staff, internal and external systems for monitoring the conduct of staff responsible for deportation escorts, measures taken following an abortive deportation attempt, etc".[254]

These investigation efforts have revealed practices used in detention and expulsion which may violate the Convention to the extent that they cause severe mental and physical suffering. Methods such as the cushion treatment (to stifle protests), which risk (and have actually caused) suffocation, the administration of drugs, the taping over of the mouth and nose, confinement in a straitjacket, handcuffing to a wheelchair or airline seat, and forcing adults to undertake long journeys wearing incontinence pads so that they do not have to be unshackled to use the toilet are all in regular use.[255] Beating and kicking by police and immigration officers have also been reported. The CPT has expressed deep concern about these practices and has recalled that "the use of force and/or means of restraint capable of causing positional asphyxia should be avoided whenever possible".[256] The CPT has also noted that the wearing of nappies "can only lead to a degrading situation" and recommended "an absolute ban on the use of means likely to obstruct the airways (nose/mouth) partially or wholly".[257] More generally, it recommended that escort staff receive specific training to reduce the risk of ill-treatment to a minimum[258] and that medical examination should be undertaken in order to document injuries and protect escort staff against unfounded allegations.

---

254 CPT's 13th General Report, CPT/Inf(2003)35, paragraph 28.

255 See Amnesty International documents: Austria – "Concerns in Europe: January-June 1999", AI Index EUR 01/002/1999; "Austria before the UN Committee against Torture: allegations of police ill-treatment", EUR 13/01/2000; Belgium – "Concerns in Europe: July-December 1999", EUR 01/001/2000; "Federal Republic of Germany: continuing pattern of police ill-treatment", EUR 23/004/1997; Spain – "Concerns in Europe: July-December 1996", EUR 01/001/1997; "Concerns in Europe: January-June 1998", EUR 01/002/1998, "Concerns in Europe: January-June 1999", EUR 01/002/1999, Switzerland, – "Concerns: July-December 1999", EUR 01/001/2000; "UK death in police custody of Joy Gardner", EUR 45/005/1995; "UK Amnesty International Report 1995"; "UK Cruel, inhuman and degrading treatment during forcible deportation", EUR 45/005/1994; *Amnesty International News*, March 2000, Col. 30, No. 2.

256 CPT's 13th General Report, CPT/Inf(2003)35, paragraph 34.

257 Ibid., paragraphs 34-36.

258 Ibid., paragraph 42.

The Court has not yet examined any complaint about these specific practices, but the jurisprudence relating to the use of force by police officers in the context of arrest relating to criminal charges is instructive. The Commission and Court have held that inhuman treatment includes such treatment as deliberately causes severe mental and physical suffering. In addition to condemning the treatment, the Court in *Ribitsch*[259] added a very strong statement that any recourse to physical force which has not been made "strictly necessary" by his own conduct diminishes human dignity as it is in principle a violation of Article 3. In *Hurtado*[260] the applicant had defecated on arrest and had been unable to change his clothes until the next day. The Commission found that such treatment was humiliating and debasing and thus in violation of Article 3. In the same case, however, they found that the applicant's having his ribs cracked by an officer kneeling on him whilst effecting the arrest was not a violation of Article 3 because of the circumstances surrounding the arrest. In *Selmouni v. France*[261] physical and psychological abuse in a police station were found to be in violation of Article 3. Reflecting the standards laid down in the UN Convention against Torture, the Court has also found that a failure by the authorities to take prompt effective measures to investigate allegations of Article 3 and to bring to justice those accused violates the "inherent procedural safeguards" of the article.[262]

The Court has considered the use of drugs in the context of the compulsory treatment of a psychiatric patient. As it was satisfied that being strapped down and subjected to the compulsory administration of drugs constituted a "therapeutic necessity in line with current medical practice",[263] it found no violation. The situation might be different where there is, as in the case of forced expulsion, no therapeutic element involved.

The Court took a decision related to the treatment of expelled asylum seekers during expulsion in *Čonka*, in which the applicants claimed they had been victims of a breach of Article 3 when the Belgian authorities forcibly wrote their aeroplane seat numbers with a ballpoint pen on their hands at the airport immediately prior to expulsion. The Court found that while writing seat numbers on the individuals' hands was particularly sensitive, it did not cross the threshold of seriousness Article 3 requires.[264]

Cases of this kind will depend on whether the treatment has reached the requisite threshold of severity required by Article 3. The concept of proportionality

---

259 *Ribitsch v. Austria*, Application No. 18896/91, judgment of 4 December 1995.

260 *Hurtado v. Switzerland*, Application No. 17549/90, judgment of 28 January 1994.

261 *Selmouni v. France*, Application No. 25803/94, judgment of 28 July 1999.

262 *Assenov v. Bulgaria*, Application No. 24760/94, judgment of 28 October 1998 and *Selmouni v. France*, Application No. 25803/94, judgment of 28 July 1999.

263 *Herczegfalvy v. Austria*, Application No. 10533/83, judgment of 24 September 1992.

264 *Čonka v. Belgium*, Application No. 51564/99, decision of 13 March 2001, paragraph 3.

which runs through all Convention case law is of particular importance in this field. In determining whether the Article 3 threshold is met, or whether the treatment falls under Article 8 (moral and physical integrity), the test will be whether the deportation could have been effected in a way which constituted less of an infringement to the dignity of the deportee. In order to determine whether there were "relevant and sufficient reasons" for the interference, the Convention demands that the state should show that other methods were investigated and rejected and that the force that was used was no more than was absolutely necessary.

Because of resistance from the airlines, and complaints by pilots, crew and other passengers travelling with forced deportees, many states have now adopted a practice of chartering planes to return illegal immigrants, and those whose asylum applications have been rejected, to their country of origin. This is now a common practice throughout Europe and has led to concerns that factors associated with the efficient economic use of the charter planes may lead to precipitate decision making in order to fill expensive empty seats.

In May 2005 the Committee of Ministers of the Council of Europe adopted "Twenty Guidelines on Forced Returns" (CM(2005)40), which are intended to address some of the worst excesses described above and to set standards for future forced returns.

Part Two – The role of the European Convention on Human Rights in situations not involving protection from expulsion

1. Detention under Article 5 and restrictions on freedom of movement under Article 2 of Protocol No. 4

Most of the asylum cases considered by the Court have related to the primary concern of the applicants to secure protection from expulsion to a situation where they would face a real risk of prohibited treatment. The related procedural safeguards have also frequently been at issue.

The restrictions imposed on asylum seekers awaiting the outcome of their applications or on those whose claims have been rejected have to date been less commonly the subject of complaints. However, this is likely to change in the future. Many of those seeking asylum in Europe now routinely face detention, often for lengthy periods and frequently in appalling conditions, or severe restrictions on their freedom of movement both whilst their claims are being processed and after their rejection but before their expulsion. The European Committee for the Prevention of Torture has criticised both the excessive and often arbitrary use of detention and the conditions in which detained asylum seekers are held.

Article 5, paragraph 1, of the ECHR sets out an exhaustive list of those situations in which an individual may be deprived of his liberty. No deprivation of liberty is permitted unless it is for one of the purposes set out in Article 5, paragraph 1.

Article 2 of Protocol No. 4 governs restrictions on freedom of movement. The permitted justifications for imposing restrictions on freedom of movement are much wider than the permissible reasons for deprivation of liberty.

The scope of the two articles is very different. Both articles are discussed below.

Deprivation of liberty or restriction on freedom of movement?

In order to decide whether or not the restrictions comply with Convention standards the first step is therefore to establish whether the factual situation in question constitutes a deprivation of liberty or a restriction on freedom of movement – that is, whether the safeguards of Article 5 or those of Article 2 of Protocol No. 4 apply in a particular case.

Whether there has been a deprivation of liberty or a restriction on movement will depend on several aspects of the specific situation. It is not simply a question of whether or not someone has been locked in a prison cell. Account needs to be taken of a whole range of criteria: the type, duration, effects and manner of implementation of the measures restricting the individual's liberty.[265]

The case of *Guzzardi v. Italy*[266] provides some guidance. The applicant had been arrested in connection with a criminal charge but the time for which he could lawfully be detained on remand had expired before the charges were ready to proceed. He was removed from the prison where he was being held and taken under court order to a small island off Sardinia to be kept under "special supervision". Whilst the island as a whole covered 50 sq. km, the area reserved for persons such as Mr Guzzardi in "compulsory residence" represented an area of not more than 2.5 sq. km. The applicant was able to move freely around this area during the day but unable to leave his dwelling between 10 p.m. and 7 a.m. He had to report twice daily to the authorities and could only leave the island with prior authorisation and under strict supervision. His contact with the outside world was also supervised and restricted. The applicant lived under these conditions for sixteen months. The Italian Government needed to succeed in its argument that he was not "deprived of his liberty" since it was unable to demonstrate that this could be justified under any of the provisions of Article 5, paragraph 1(a)-(f).

The Court stated that it was not possible to establish a deprivation of liberty on the strength of any one aspect of his regime taken individually, but *taken cumulatively and in combination*, in the light of the factors set out above, it considered that the applicant had been deprived of his liberty and his case was to be examined under Article 5 rather than Article 2 of Protocol No. 4.

In contrast, in the case of *Raimondo v. Italy*,[267] "special police supervision" meant that the applicant could not leave his own home without informing the police but did not require their permission to do so. He was under an obligation to report to the police on certain days and also to stay at his home between 9 p.m. and 7 a.m. every night. The Court held that these restrictions were not a deprivation of liberty and should only be considered as a restriction on freedom of movement. Article 5 did not therefore apply.

The Court also had to examine this issue in the case of *Amuur v. France*.[268] A group of asylum seekers from Somalia who had arrived at the Paris-Orly Airport

---

265 The terms "deprivation of liberty" and "detention" are used interchangeably in this book.

266 Application No. 7367/76, judgment of 2 October 1980.

267 Application No. 12954/87, judgment of 22 February 1994.

268 Application No. 19776/92, judgment of 25 June 1996.

via Syria were held for twenty days in the international transit zone and a nearby hotel specifically adapted for holding asylum seekers. In this case the Court noted in particular:

> "Holding aliens in the international zone does indeed involve a restriction upon liberty [of movement], but one which is not in every respect comparable to that which obtains in centres for the detention of aliens pending deportation. Such confinement, accompanied by suitable safeguards for the persons concerned, is acceptable only in order to enable States to prevent unlawful immigration whilst complying with their international obligations, particularly under the 1951 Geneva Convention Relating to the Status of Refugees and the European Convention on Human Rights. States' legitimate concern to foil the increasingly frequent attempts to get round immigration restrictions must not deprive asylum seekers of the protection afforded by these Conventions."

The Court further stated that many Council of Europe member states were faced with an increasing flow of asylum seekers, and that it was aware of the difficulties involved in the reception of asylum seekers at most large European airports. States had the sovereign right to control aliens' entry into and residence in their territory, but in doing so, the Court reminded them, the provisions of the Convention, including Article 5, had to be respected.

As in the *Guzzardi* case, in deciding whether there was a deprivation of liberty or a restriction of movement, the type, duration, effects and manner of the measure in question had to be examined. The Court discussed whether there had been a restriction on liberty of movement or a deprivation of liberty. It decided that this was an issue of "degree and intensity". The applicants had been held at the airport for twenty days. They were under constant police surveillance, and for most of the time not provided with any legal or social assistance. As in *Guzzardi*, the government had argued that there was no deprivation of liberty, only a restriction on freedom of movement. The government suggested that the applicants could at any time have removed themselves from the sphere of application of the measure in question, arguing that the transit zone was "closed on the French side" but "open to the outside".

The Court held[269] that the mere fact that it was possible for asylum seekers to leave the country where they wished to seek refuge did not mean that there had not been a "restriction on liberty". (The use of the word "restriction" rather than "deprivation" is odd, as no complaint had been made under Article 2 of Protocol No. 4.) The possibility became theoretical if no other country offered protection comparable to that which they expected to find in the country where they were seeking asylum. In addition, in the case of *Amuur*, sending the applicants back to Syria in fact only became possible following negotiations between the French and Syrian authorities, and they had not been free to leave whenever they wanted as was alleged by the government. The Court therefore concluded that the applicants' detention in the transit zone amounted to a deprivation of liberty and that Article 5 was applicable.

---

269 Paragraph 48.

It is clear from this case law that an order that a person should reside in a particular place will not be enough to amount to a deprivation of liberty so as to attract the very stringent protection of Article 5. This is so even if it includes a night curfew (see *Cyprus v. Turkey*)[270] coupled with daytime reporting requirements such as those in *Raimondo*. However, the closed and cut-off nature of such a restriction, coupled with its duration, might make it a deprivation of liberty rather than a mere restriction on freedom of movement.

In *H.M. v. Switzerland*[271] the placing of an elderly lady, who could no longer care for herself and was unwilling to co-operate with home help, in a home which she could leave in theory but not in practice was held by a majority not to be a deprivation of liberty. In *Riera Blume*[272] in contrast, the applicant children who were confined – with the connivance of the police – with their families in a hotel in order to debrief them from the sect they had been with, had been deprived of their liberty. In *Laments v. Latvia*,[273] house arrest without the possibility to leave was held to constitute a deprivation of liberty rather than a restriction on freedom of movement.[274] Likewise in *Mancini v. Italy*[275] house arrest, which required the accused to obtain the permission of the authorities to leave and not just to give notification as in *Raimondo*, was a deprivation of liberty.

The distinction between the two types of restriction is of absolutely fundamental importance since the Convention provisions which apply are fundamentally, and in some respects surprisingly, different.

Detention under Article 5 of the Convention – The right to liberty and security of the person

Article 5, paragraph 1, of the European Convention states that:

> "1. Everyone has the right to liberty and security of person. No one shall be deprived of his liberty save in the following cases and in accordance with a procedure prescribed by law:
>
> (a) the lawful detention of a person after conviction by a competent court;
>
> (b) the lawful arrest or detention of a person for non-compliance with the lawful order of a court or in order to secure the fulfilment of any obligation prescribed by law;

---

270 Applications Nos. 6780/74 and 6950/75, Commission decision of 26 May 1975. Decision on the law found in Commission Report (1976) EHRR 482.

271 Application No. 39187/98, judgment of 26 February 2002.

272 *Riera Blume and Others v. Spain*, Application No. 37680/97, judgment of 14 January 2000.

273 Application No. 58442/00, judgment of 28 November 2002.

274 Application No. 44955/98, judgment of 2 August 2001.

275 Application No. 44955/98, judgment of 2 August 2001.

(c) the lawful arrest or detention of a person effected for the purpose of bringing him before the competent legal authority on reasonable suspicion of having committed an offence or when it is reasonably considered necessary to prevent his committing an offence or fleeing after having done so;

(d) the detention of a minor by lawful order for the purpose of educational supervision or his lawful detention for the purpose of bringing him before the competent legal authority;

(e) the lawful detention of persons for the prevention of the spreading of infectious diseases, of persons of unsound mind, alcoholics and drug addicts or vagrants;

(f) the lawful arrest or detention of a person to prevent his effecting an unauthorised entry into the country or of a person against whom action is being taken with a view to deportation or extradition."

Deprivation of liberty is only lawful if it is for one of the specified purposes. A detention which is not for an identified purpose covered by Article 5, paragraph 1(a)-(f), is automatically unlawful.

Article 5 of the European Convention on Human Rights is aimed at preventing arbitrary deprivation of liberty.

"Arbitrary" detention

The protection afforded by Article 5 is available to prevent detention being "arbitrary" but the Convention organs are yet to provide a coherent definition of what arbitrariness entails. The ECHR is not unique in this respect and the Working Group on Arbitrary Detention (established by the UN Commission on Human Rights) has recognised that the UDHR and ICCPR do not definitively answer the question of what constitutes arbitrary detention either.[276] The working group adopted a pragmatic approach to this question, seemingly guided by Resolution 1997/50, which stated that a deprivation of liberty would not be arbitrary if it was the result of a final judicial decision carried out in accordance with domestic law and, importantly, it did not run counter to international standards. Furthermore, it classified arbitrary detention as falling within the following situations:

(a) where there is no possible and clear legal basis to justify the detention;

(b) where persons are detained because they have been exercising other Convention rights;

(c) where the right to fair trial is abrogated wholly or partially; or

(d) where detention is of such a grave nature it possesses an arbitrary character.

---

276 See E/CN.4/1998/44 and E/CN.4/2000/4. Reports and more information on working group see www.ohchr.org/english/issues/detention/index.htm

The UN Human Rights Committee (UNHRC) has also confirmed that "arbitrary" means something more than merely "against the law" and the term must be "interpreted more broadly to include such elements as inappropriateness and injustice".[277]

Purpose and justification

It is the prohibition on arbitrariness which is meant by the word "security" in Article 5, paragraph 1. It requires that every arrest or detention is lawful, both substantially and procedurally. In addition to the UN working group's definition this means that it has in fact been carried out for one of the six specified reasons in Article 5, paragraph 1(a)-(f). This is an exhaustive list of circumstances, which will justify detention. If the arrest or detention has not taken place for one of the purposes set out in Article 5, it is automatically a breach of the Convention.

In many states it appears that aliens crossing or seeking to cross the borders of states are detained in a fairly unpredictable fashion and for a variety of purposes. They are often not informed as to why they are arrested and detained. They are not informed of the legal rules authorising their detention.

People in more or less similar circumstances who may ask the reason for their detention are often given several different answers: they have not proved their identity; they have crossed the border unlawfully; they are awaiting deportation; or they are not residing at a registered address.

Such a framework needs to be clear and transparent so those like legal situations are dealt with in a like manner.[278]

Since Article 5 requires that a deprivation of liberty must be for one of the purposes set out in Article 5, paragraph 1(a)-(f), the detaining authorities must have clearly identified which of the purposes under Article 5, paragraph 1(a)-(f), justifies the deprivation of liberty.

This is crucial because if the detaining authority has not directed its mind to the genuine, specific purpose of detention, it will be less likely to have appreciated other procedural rights which such detention entails.

In addition the detainee must **always** be informed of the **purpose and justification** of his detention, as well as the applicable national law which authorises it (see further below on procedural safeguards). In *Shamsa v. Poland*[279] the Court found a violation precisely because the national law under which they were held pending the execution of the expulsion decision was unclear.

---

277 See *A. v. Australia*, No. 560/1993, which was reaffirmed in *Danyal Shafiq v. Australia*, No. 1324/2004, paragraph 7.2. More on the jurisprudence of the UNHRC below at page 87.

278 The United Kingdom is the only member state that has felt compelled to derogate from Article 5 in order to detain foreigners it cannot expel.

279 Application No. 45355/99, judgment of 27 November 2003.

A number of situations might justify an asylum seeker's deprivation of liberty under Article 5, paragraph 1(a)-(f).

Establishing someone's identity

Article 5, paragraph 1(b), provides for detention in the following case:

> "the lawful arrest or detention of a person for non-compliance with the lawful order of a court or in order to secure the fulfilment of any obligation prescribed by law".

The first part of this provision relates only to orders of a court, not of a prosecutor or any part of the executive. Immigration detainees are rarely held for non-compliance with a lawful order of a court.

It is the second limb of this provision, which provides for detention in order to secure the fulfilment of any obligation prescribed by law, that may be relevant here. It concerns only cases where the law:

(i) imposes an obligation to prove identity; and

(ii) permits the detention of a person to compel him/her to fulfil this specific and concrete obligation.

Detention cannot be justified on the basis of a general duty of obedience to the law. If there is a duty under domestic law to prove identity when asked by the authorities, and a person is unwilling or unable to do so, the provisions of domestic law may make detention lawful under Article 5, paragraph 1(b). However, if it becomes clear that the person detained remains unable to prove his/her identity, there have to be procedural safeguards in place to ensure the detention is not prolonged indefinitely.

The provisions of Article 5, paragraph 1(b), do not cover situations where a person is detained as a sanction for failure to comply; that is only lawful when there has been a court order. It only authorises detention to secure compliance.

Crossing the border unlawfully

Article 5, paragraph 1(c), provides for detention in the following situation:

> "the lawful arrest or detention of a person effected for the purpose of bringing him before the competent legal authority on reasonable suspicion of having committed an offence or when it is reasonably considered necessary to prevent his committing an offence or fleeing after having done so".

This provision only applies in situations where the individual is detained in connection with criminal or administrative proceedings relating to the offence of irregular border crossings. Under this provision deprivation of liberty may be lawful in situations:

(i) where the person appears to have committed the offence of illegally crossing the border into the detaining state;

(ii) where there are reasonable fears he/she will try to do so if released;

(iii) where there are reasonable fears he/she appears to have committed the offence and will flee before criminal proceedings can be brought.

Detention under this provision must – both initially and continuously – remain linked to one of the three specified factors and the relevant factor must be specified to the detainee. It must also be "for the purpose of bringing him before a competent authority" and must therefore be linked to the prosecution of the relevant criminal law or administrative offence.

The detention must always be necessary if it is to prevent the commission of the offence or to prevent absconding.

If the detainee is released without charge, the arrest on reasonable suspicion of having committed the offence will not necessarily violate Article 5 provided that the arrest had genuinely been made for that purpose. However, this is only true for the initial period of the detention. The legality of continued detention depends on whether the reasonable suspicion persists and, much more importantly, whether prosecution for the criminal or administrative offence is actually under way. The detention will cease to be lawful if the link to the reason why the person was arrested is not kept alive by the diligent pursuit of the relevant criminal/administrative proceedings. In *Ciulla v. Italy*[280] the applicant was detained in order that a compulsory residence order of the kind which featured in the *Guzzardi* and *Raimondo* cases, described above, could be made. The Court found there was no link with intended criminal proceedings so as to justify the detention under Article 5, paragraph 1(c).

Vagrants

Article 5, paragraph 1(e), allows for detention in the following cases:

> "the lawful detention of persons for the prevention of the spreading of infectious diseases, of persons of unsound mind, alcoholics or drug addicts or vagrants".

Asylum seekers and other migrants who have no visible means of support might fall into the category of "vagrants". They may even give themselves up voluntarily to the authorities because of this. The case of *De Wilde, Ooms and Versyp v. Belgium*[281] made it clear that whilst vagrancy may justify a short proportionate detention, even such voluntary surrender will not absolve states from their requirement to observe the procedural safeguards of Article 5.

The Court made it clear in the case of *Litwa v. Poland*[282] that the detention in a sobering-up centre of someone found apparently drunk must not only be for the purpose of sobering up, but it must also be necessary – that is, that a less invasive interference would not suffice.

---

280 Application No. 1152/84, judgment of 22 February 1989.

281 Applications Nos. 2832/66, 2865/66 and 2899/66, judgment of 18 June 1971.

282 Application No. 26629/95, judgment of 4 April 2000.

Preventing unauthorised entry or pending deportation

The one immigration situation which is expressly provided for in Article 5 is that of

> "the lawful arrest or detention of a person to prevent his effecting an unauthorised entry into the country or of a person against whom action is being taken with a view to deportation or extradition".

This provision applies in two situations:

(i) detention to prevent a person entering a country unlawfully; and

(ii) detention whilst a person is awaiting the execution of a decision to deport or extradite him/her.

The Court has recently held by four votes to three in the case of *Saadi v. the United Kingdom*[283] that a person can be detained to prevent him effecting an unauthorised entry at any stage before he has been granted leave to remain in the country. Even if it is accepted that he has, in the words of one judge, "no intention to effect an authorised entry", shown no risk of absconding, surrendered himself to the immigration authorities, and been granted temporary residence whilst the asylum claim is being processed, according to the Chamber judgment, Article 5, paragraph 1(f), in principle still authorises such detention.

At the time of writing, *Saadi* was due to be heard by the Grand Chamber.

The issue in *Saadi* is not only whether a person who is properly and diligently following the prescribed procedures for making a claim for asylum is a person who is seeking to "effect an unauthorised entry". Although the two limbs of Article 5, paragraph 1(f), are slightly different, the further important question that arose in *Saadi* is whether the test of reasonable necessity applies to these two types of detention.

The Court has always held that compliance with Article 5, paragraph 1(b) (*Vasileva v. Denmark*),[284] paragraph 1(c) (*Jecius v. Lithuania*[285] and *Mansur v. Turkey*)[286] and paragraph 1(e) (*Litwa v. Poland*)[287] requires not only that the detention should be for the specified purpose but that an individual assessment of the necessity of the detention must be made, and the necessity demonstrated.

In *Saadi v. the United Kingdom*, the Court also considered, for the first time, whether the same test of necessity applies when asylum seekers are detained pending the determination of their claims.

---

283 Application No. 1329/03, judgment of 11 July 2006.

284 Application No. 52792/99, judgment of 25 September 2003.

285 Application No. 34578/97, judgment of 31 July 2000.

286 Application No. 16026/90, judgment of 8 June 1995.

287 Application No. 26629/95, judgment of 4 April 2000.

The Chamber found (by four votes to three) that a short period of detention (seven days) whilst a "fast track" asylum application was being processed did not have to meet any test of necessity. (The detention in question was for those who could not otherwise have been detained as they were expressly recognised not to pose any risk of absconding.) The majority of the Chamber found:

> "All that is required is that the detention should be a genuine part of the process to determine whether the individual should be granted immigration clearance and/or asylum and that it should not otherwise be arbitrary, for example on account of its length."

Having adopted that position of principle – that the necessity test applicable under Article 5, paragraph 1(b)-(e), did not apply to immigration detention – it did not therefore consider that it was necessary to examine whether the kind of restriction on freedom of movement that was imposed in *Raimondo* might have sufficed to meet the administrative needs of the United Kingdom authorities. Such restrictions need not have involved a deprivation of liberty as defined by the Court.

In *Saadi* the Court was applying to applicants for asylum the same approach as it had previously taken towards those whose requests to enter or remain had been rejected and who were being detained in the context of the execution of a judicially determined expulsion, or those detained in the context of extradition proceedings.

The Court had already held in the case of *Chahal v. the United Kingdom*[288] that the test of necessity does not have to be applied to those detained after a decision to refuse the entry or to deport them has been taken. However, detention under this provision requires expulsion proceedings to be in progress and to be prosecuted with due diligence. *Chahal* concerned the proposed deportation on national security grounds of a Sikh activist. The Court found no violation as a result of the extended detention as the United Kingdom was able to demonstrate that its courts had acted with due diligence in dealing with the many proceedings which the applicant himself had initiated to challenge his expulsion.

In *Quinn v. France*,[289] on the other hand, the Court found Article 5 to have been violated because the detention lacked proportionality and the state had not conducted the relevant proceedings with due diligence. In *Singh v. Czech Republic*[290] the detention was held to violate Article 5, paragraph 1(f), because the Czech authorities had failed to exercise due diligence in pursuing the necessary documentation from the Indian authorities to effect the return to that country.

---

288 Application No. 22414/93, judgment of 15 November 1996.

289 Application No. 18680/91, judgment of 22 March 1995.

290 Application No. 60538/00, judgment of 25 January 2005.

In *Ali v. Switzerland*[291] the Swiss similarly wanted to extradite the applicant to Somalia, but could not as he had no travel document. Since the extradition was thus impossible, the detention could no longer be regarded as being with a view to extradition.[292]

The UN Human Rights Committee has considered the question of necessity and the detention of asylum seekers under the corresponding provisions of the ICCPR. Their approach is relevant to any interpretation or application of the ECHR under Article 53 (see introduction above). The UN Human Rights Committee has examined a number of complaints against Australia,[293] where the relevant legislation foresaw the arrest and detention of everyone who fell within a specified sub-group of unlawful non-citizens without examination of their individual and specific personal circumstances. The committee emphasised that the concept of arbitrariness could not simply be equated with "against the law" but must also include such elements as "inappropriateness and injustice" and, importantly, that custody could be considered arbitrary "if not necessary in all the circumstances of the case".

Article 18 of the EU Procedures Directive (which must be transposed by all EU member states by 1 December 2007) stipulates that member states shall not hold a person in detention for the sole reason that he/she is an applicant for asylum.

As noted above, the case of *Saadi* has now been accepted for reconsideration by the Grand Chamber.

Prescribed by law

As is clear from the text, the arrest must be lawful according to domestic law and in that sense too cannot be arbitrary. The Court found a violation of this provision in the case of *Bozano v. France*.[294] An Italian citizen who had been convicted in his absence of murder by an Italian court was forcibly taken at night by French police to the Swiss border. He was handed over into Swiss police custody following what transpired to be an unlawful deportation order, drawn up to circumvent the French court's ruling that extradition could not take place. The Court held the deprivation of liberty to be arbitrary in motivation and unlawful. The detention appeared to be for the purpose of deportation but was in reality a disguised illegal extradition.

---

291 Application No. 24881/94, judgment of 5 August 1998.

292 See also *Singh v. Czech Republic*, Application No. 60538/00, judgment of 25 January 2005.

293 *A. v. Australia*, No. 560/1993, *C. v. Australia*, No. 900/1999, *Baban v. Australia*, No. 1014/2001, *Bakhtiyari v. Australia*, No. 1069/2002. The principles in *A.*, adopted in 1997, have been subsequently reaffirmed in *Danyal Shafiq v. Australia*, No. 1324/2004, adopted on 13 November 2006.

294 Application No. 9990/82, judgment of 18 December 1986.

As can be seen from the first sentence of Article 5, any deprivation of liberty must not only be for a purpose authorised by Article 5, paragraph 1(a)-(f). It must also be in accordance with a procedure prescribed by law in order to be lawful under the Convention. As the Court stated in the case of *Amuur v. France*, this primarily requires any arrest or detention to have a legal basis in domestic law. However, the domestic law must meet Convention standards. The Court went on to state:

> "10. However, these words do not merely refer back to domestic law; like the expressions 'in accordance with the law' and 'prescribed by law' in the second paragraphs of Articles 8 to 11, they also relate to the quality of the law, requiring it to be compatible with the rule of law, a concept inherent in all the Articles of the Convention."

Quality of law, in this context, means that a law which authorises deprivation of liberty must be sufficiently **precise and accessible** to avoid all risk of arbitrariness.

The Court emphasised in *Amuur v. France* that this is especially the case in respect of a vulnerable foreign asylum seeker. This, the Court said, was of fundamental importance with regard to asylum seekers at airports, particularly in view of the need to reconcile the protection of fundamental rights with the requirements of states' immigration policies. It can be assumed that the Court would consider the situation at other important ports of entry into a state in a similar manner.

In *Amuur*, the detainees were not being held under a clearly identifiable legal regime. Although there were French regulations in force at the time, these did not treat the detainees either as having entered France or as having been deprived of their liberty. None of the applicable rules allowed ordinary courts to review the conditions under which they were held or if necessary to impose a limit on the administrative authorities as regards the length of time for which they were held. In particular, the rules did not provide for legal, humanitarian and social assistance. The Court therefore found that the rules did not sufficiently guarantee the applicants' right to liberty, and there had been a violation of the requirement of Article 5, paragraph 1, that any deprivation of liberty must be in accordance with a procedure prescribed by law.

This requirement of lawfulness, inherent in Article 5, paragraph 1, is separate from the procedural requirements set out in Article 5, paragraphs 2–5, described below.

Procedural guarantees under Article 5 of the Convention

Article 5, paragraphs 2–5, set out the procedural rights that detainees must be afforded, once it has been established that they have lawfully been deprived of their liberty. What follows will very briefly outline these rights.

Article 5, paragraph 2, stipulates:

> "Everyone who is arrested shall be informed promptly, in a language which he understands, of the reasons for his arrest and of any charge against him."

The Court has interpreted this provision as meaning that any arrested person must be told, in simple, non-technical language that he can understand, the essential legal and factual grounds for his arrest, so that he/she can, if necessary, apply to a court to challenge its lawfulness.[295]

In the *Saadi* case referred to above, although the Court found no violation of Article 5, paragraph 1(f), it did find a violation of Article 5, paragraph 2. The reason for the applicant's detention was administrative convenience for the processing of fast track claims, but he was given no reasons at all for seventy-six hours after he was detained. The Court found that "general statements – parliamentary announcements in the present case – cannot replace the need for the individual to be informed of the reason for his arrest and detention".

In *Shamayev and Others v. Georgia and Russia*[296] the Court found a violation of Article 5, paragraph 2, in an extradition case where the applicants were given no reasons for their detention for four days.

Article 5, paragraph 3, states:

> "Everyone arrested or detained in accordance with the provisions of paragraph 1.c of this article shall be brought promptly before a judge or other officer authorised by law to exercise judicial power and shall be entitled to trial within a reasonable time or to release pending trial. Release may be conditioned by guarantees to appeal for trial."

This provision only applies to those who are detained under Article 5, paragraph 1(c), in connection with criminal proceedings being taken against them.

Those detained under other procedures do not have to have their detention ordered by a judge, but they must have access to a judge to challenge the lawfulness of the detention.

Article 5, paragraph 4, states:

> "Everyone who is deprived of his liberty by arrest or detention shall be entitled to take proceedings by which the lawfulness of his detention shall be decided speedily by a court and his release ordered if the detention is not lawful."

Article 5, paragraph 4, not only requires access to a judge to have the initial lawfulness of the detention decided but also requires access to regular periodic reviews, by a court, of the need for continued detention.

Article 18, paragraph 2, of the EU Procedures Directive provides that all detainees must have the possibility of speedy judicial review of their detention.

---

295 *Fox, Campbell and Hartley v. the United Kingdom*, Applications Nos. 12244/86, 12245/86 and 12383/86, judgment of 30 August 1990.

296 Application No. 366378/02, judgment of 12 April 2005.

Article 5, paragraph 5, stipulates:

> "Everyone who has been the victim of arrest or detention in contravention of the provisions of this article shall have an enforceable right to compensation."

The importance which the Convention attaches to the right of liberty is demonstrated by the fact that this is one of only two provisions of the Convention which provide a direct express right to compensation by national authorities for Convention violations.[297] For the European Court to find a violation of Article 5, paragraph 5, there must be a finding of a violation of one or more other elements of Article 5. The violation can either be of the procedural safeguards in Article 5, paragraphs 2-4, or of the substantive provisions of Article 5, paragraph 1.

Lawyers and NGOs working in this field should be vigilant in holding states accountable for violations of Article 5 and be aware that there is a right for compensation to be awarded if they have occurred.[298]

Detention conditions

The prohibition on torture on inhuman or degrading treatment or punishment contained in Article 3 has already been considered in the context of persons facing the threat of expulsion to face such prohibited treatment.

The Court has now held in a number of cases that the conditions in which detainees are held or the severity of the regimes to which they are subjected may violate Article 3. The first judgments on this point, *Dougoz v. Greece* and *Peers v. Greece*,[299] both related to immigration detention. In the case of *Dougoz v. Greece* the applicant was detained whilst awaiting expulsion to Syria. He complained to the European Court about the conditions of his detention. He alleged, *inter alia,* that he was confined in an overcrowded and dirty cell with insufficient sanitary and sleeping facilities, scarce hot water, no fresh air or natural daylight and no yard in which to exercise. It was even impossible for him to read a book because his cell was so overcrowded.

The Court noted that conditions of detention may sometimes amount to inhuman or degrading treatment. When assessing conditions of detention, account had to be taken of the cumulative effects of these conditions, as well as of specific allegations made by the applicant. It was noted that the applicant's allegations were corroborated by reports from the European Committee for the Prevention

---

297 The other is Article 3 of Protocol No. 7 relating to miscarriages of justice.

298 Under EU law the right to compensation is not limited in this way. Failure to transpose any directive or to implement it correctly can give rise to an action in damages against the state brought by individuals who are adversely affected by the failure. See *Francovich and Bonifaci v. Italy,* C-6 and 9/90 [1991] ECR I-5357.

299 Application No. 40907/98, judgment of 6 March 2001.

of Torture.[300] The Court considered that the conditions of the applicant's detention, in combination with the fact that he had been detained in these conditions for eighteen months, amounted to a violation of Article 3 of the Convention.

The case of *Kalashnikov v. the Russian Federation*[301] concerned an applicant who had been held in appalling conditions for five years, mainly in pre-trial detention. His cell measured 17 square metres and contained eight bunk beds. It nearly always held 24 inmates – there were three men to every bunk and the inmates had to sleep in turn. There was a toilet in the cell, and the person using the toilet was in view of both his cell mates and the prison guard. The cell had no ventilation and was overrun with cockroaches and ants. The applicant contracted a variety of skin diseases and fungal infections, losing his toenails and some of his fingernails.

Not surprisingly, the Court found these conditions to clearly violate Article 3 of the Convention. It accepted that there was no indication that there was a positive intention of humiliating or debasing the applicant, but the absence of any such purpose could not exclude a finding of a breach of the Convention. The Court has since on a number of occasions made similar findings in relation to conditions of detention or prison regimes.[302]

In July 2006 the Court made a rare fact-finding visit to the detention centre in Larissa in Greece where the applicant had been held for three months pending expulsion. Having noted that the physical conditions appeared to be acceptable (the cells in question had been cleaned and freshly painted just prior to the Court's visit), the Court nevertheless considered that the general conditions – for example, cramped space, absence of exercise facilities, no TV or radio – were unsuitable for anything more that the shortest of detentions. The judgment referred to the CPT recommendations on police detention.[303]

In *Mubilanzila Mayeka and Kaniki Mitunga v. Belgium*[304] a 5 year-old child was held without any accompanying family in an adult detention centre. The Court had no difficulty in finding a violation of Article 3. It noted that the child's very young age, the vulnerable position in which she was placed (which resulted in considerable distress) and the circumstances of her deportation would have caused her extreme anxiety. Leaving this 5 year-old girl in an adult detention centre and failing to take steps for the child to receive childcare

---

300 More on the work of this committee below.

301 Application No. 47095/99, judgment of 15 July 2002.

302 See, for example, *Peers v. Greece*, Application No. 28524/95, judgment of 19 April 2001, and *Van der Ven v. the Netherlands*, Application No. 50901/99, judgment of 4 February 2003.

303 *Kaja v. Greece*, Application No. 32927/03, judgment of 27 July 2006, citing CPT General Report, 3 September 2002.

304 Application No. 13178/03, judgment of 12 October 2006.

during and after the deportation displayed a complete lack of humanity towards a child of her age and situation and, as such, amounted to inhuman treatment within Article 3.

The European Committee for the Prevention of Torture and Inhuman or Degrading Treatment or Punishment

In the cases of *Dougoz* and *Kalashnikov* the Court relied on reports issued by the European Committee for the Prevention of Torture and Inhuman or Degrading Treatment or Punishment (the CPT) when finding the first violations of Article 3 of the Convention in relation to prison conditions.

Concerns that violations of Article 3 should be prevented, and not merely condemned after they have occurred, inspired the drafting, in 1987, of the European Convention for the Prevention of Torture and Inhuman or Degrading Treatment or Punishment. The convention provides for non-judicial preventive machinery to protect detainees. It is based on a system of visits by the CPT. The CPT's members are independent and impartial experts from a variety of backgrounds, for example lawyers, medical doctors and specialists in prison or police matters. The CPT visits places of detention (for example, prisons and juvenile detention centres, police stations, holding centres for immigration detainees and psychiatric hospitals), to see how persons deprived of their liberty are treated and, if necessary, to recommend improvements to states.

CPT delegations visit contracting states periodically, but additional "ad hoc" visits can also be arranged if necessary. The committee must notify the state concerned of its presence on the territory but does not have to specify the exact time of the visit or give advance notice of which establishments it will visit.

The CPT delegations must be given unlimited access to places of detention and the right to move inside such places without restriction. They interview persons deprived of their liberty in private and communicate freely with anyone who can provide information. The recommendations which the CPT draw up on the basis of the visits are included in a report which is sent to the state concerned. These reports are confidential unless the state agrees to their publication. However, if a country fails to co-operate or refuses to improve the situation in the light of the committee's recommendations, the CPT may decide to make a public statement. In addition, the CPT draws up a general report on its activities every year, which is made public.

Over its years of activity in the field, the CPT has developed standards relating to the treatment of persons deprived of their liberty. These standards have been published and can be found on the committee's website, www.cpt.coe. int. Individuals, lawyers, NGOs and other persons who are concerned about suspected ill-treatment or detention conditions can approach the CPT and bring their concerns to the committee's attention. As explained above, the CPT can arrange ad hoc visits and does rely on information received from the public in planning its work.

The CPT has commented extensively and critically not only on the physical conditions, but also on the arbitrariness of the detention, and on the absence of legal safeguards and restrictive regimes under which immigration detainees are frequently held. It noted in many cases that those conditions and regimes are significantly worse than those which exist within the mainstream criminal justice system.

Restrictions on freedom of movement

Many of those who are either seeking asylum or whose claims have been rejected and who are awaiting expulsion are not detained in the sense that they are deprived of their liberty so as to attract the protection of Article 5. They are, however, often subject to severe restrictions on their freedom of movement.

The right to freedom of movement is contained in Article 2, paragraph 1, of Protocol No. 4: "Everyone lawfully within the territory of a state shall within that territory have the right to liberty of movement and freedom to choose his residence."

As can be seen from the text of this provision, freedom of movement applies only to persons lawfully within the territory. Those unlawfully within the territory have no such right. There appears, therefore, to be a lacuna in the law. Restrictions – not amounting to deprivation of liberty – appear to be able to be imposed at will on those who are not lawfully within the territory under this provision, though issues might arise in relation to Article 8. Respect for personal autonomy is guaranteed under the private life rubric of that article. The protection of Article 8 is not restricted to those lawfully within the territory but applies, under Article 1, to everyone within the jurisdiction.

This requirement of lawfulness primarily refers to domestic law, which may lay down certain criteria that have to be fulfilled. So an alien who has had his/her residence permit revoked, or who has not complied with certain conditions of admission, may not be able to rely on this provision. In the case of *Sulejmanovic and Others v. Italy*,[305] the applicants were unable to benefit from the comparable provisions relating to lawful residence found in Protocol No. 7 as they had not made a request for refugee status to be recognised.

States are, however, prohibited from classifying as unlawful in their domestic law the exercise of any Convention right. Since the right to seek and enjoy asylum from persecution is a right enshrined in international law and the right to have access to the protection determination procedures is expressly guaranteed in the Convention jurisprudence (see above), those who have made an asylum application are "lawfully" on the territory until such time as that application has been definitively rejected.

---

305 Applications Nos. 57574/00 and 57575/00, judgment of 8 November 2002.

In a very old case, *Paramanathan v. Germany*,[306] the Commission considered that a breach of residence conditions deprived the asylum seeker's presence in the territory of its lawfulness. However, in Germany's 5th Periodic Report,[307] submitted for consideration by the UN Human Rights Committee, the state party noted that in Germany, although an asylum seeker's right to reside does not constitute a residence permit, it does, for the duration of the asylum procedure, provide "lawful residence" and that such persons are thus brought within the scope of Article 12, paragraph 1, of the covenant (the relevant provision of which is identically worded to that of Article 2 of Protocol No. 4 of the ECHR).[308]

Article 2 of Protocol No. 4 is a qualified right.

Paragraphs 3 and 4 of this provision read:

> "3. No restrictions shall be placed on the exercise of these rights other than such as are in accordance with law and are necessary in a democratic society in the interests of national security and public safety, for the maintenance of *ordre public*, for the prevention of crime, for the protection of health and morals, or for the protection of the rights and freedoms of others.
>
> 4. The rights set forth in paragraph 1 may also be subject, in particular areas, to restrictions imposed in accordance with law and justified by the public interest in a democratic society."

As with all qualified rights in the Convention, the Court examines issues under this provision by asking a number of questions.

First, the Court examines the nature of the right, that is, if the provision is applicable to the present situation.

Second, it considers whether there has been an interference with that right.

Third, if there has been an interference, the Court moves on to examine whether this interference can be justified under paragraphs 3 and 4. In order for the interference to be justified, it has to be in accordance with the law. As has been discussed above under the section on Article 5, this does not only mean that there has to be national law allowing the interference, but there also has to be a certain quality to this law. The law has to be precise and ascertainable, so that an individual can regulate his/her conduct by it (if need be with legal advice).

Fourth, the interference has to pursue a legitimate aim, that is, has to be for one of the reasons set out in paragraphs 3 and 4.

---

306 Application No. 12068/86, decision of 1 December 1986, 51 DR 237.

307 CCPR/C/DEU/2002/5, 4 December 2002.

308 Article 7 of the EU Procedures Directive, which must be transposed into all member states' national law by 1 December 2007, provides for an EU law right to remain on the territory pending the examination of the application, but states that this right shall not constitute a residence permit.

Fifth and finally, the interference – the restriction on freedom of movement – must be necessary in a democratic society. This means it has to correspond to a pressing social need and, most importantly, be proportionate to the legitimate aim pursued. The concept of proportionality has been mentioned above and is one that lies at the heart of the Convention. Whether or not an interference is proportionate will depend on all the circumstances of the case. It needs to be examined if relevant and sufficient reasons have been advanced for the interference, if procedural safeguards were in place and if the interference impaired the very essence of the right.

In its General Comment No. 27 on Freedom of Movement the UN Human Rights Committee stated that "the application of restriction in any individual case must be based on clear legal grounds and meet the test of necessity and the requirements of proportionality".[309]

If the Chamber judgment in *Saadi* were to be upheld by the Grand Chamber the paradoxical result would be that restrictions on freedom of movement imposed on asylum seekers do have to meet the necessity test, but the much more serious interference of a deprivation of liberty does not.

In the case of *Raimondo v. Italy*, referred to above, special supervision measures were imposed on the applicant, who was suspected of mafia crimes. The Court held that in view of the threat posed by the mafia to a democratic society, there were legitimate aims to maintain *ordre public* and prevent crime. The supervision measures were considered as necessary until they were revoked by the national courts. However, there was a violation of Article 2 of Protocol No. 4 since the authorities had not acted with due diligence in implementing the decision to revoke the measures.

The EU Reception Conditions Directive (Article 7) regulates the conditions which are to apply to restrictions imposed on freedom of movement. It specifically provides that applicants cannot be required to obtain permission to keep appointments with authorities and courts if their appearance is necessary.

A number of cases against Germany concerning the restrictive application of Article 2 of Protocol No. 4 to asylum seekers in that state are currently pending before the ECtHR.[310]

2. Family life and private life

The relevance of Article 8's private life rubric (the right to respect for moral and physical integrity) has already been looked at in the context of protection from expulsion. Because of the protracted duration of asylum determination

---

309 CCPR/C/21Rev/Add9, paragraphs 15-16.

310 See, for example, *Omwenyeke v. Germany*, Application No. 44294/04.

procedures, many asylum seekers will have formed personal and even family relationships in the state where protection was sought by the time their claims are finally rejected.

The second situation in which Article 8 may be relevant therefore concerns the interference with family or private life relationships which can occur when the state seeks to implement a decision to expel an individual whose claim to be in need of international protection has been rejected.

Article 8 may also be relevant in situations where one family member's need for international protection has been recognised and other family members – who may not have such a need in their own right – either seek to remain with, or to join, the protected individual on the basis of their relationship to that person.[311]

The notion of "family life"

The Court has repeatedly asserted that the Convention does not guarantee aliens a right of entry or residence in a particular country, and whilst expulsion cases concern family life, they also concern immigration and states retain the right under international law to regulate such matters.[312] However, where an individual has close family ties or an established family unit in one country, the removal of that individual may amount to a violation of Article 8.[313] Likewise the refusal to permit family members overseas to join an individual who has been granted international protection will also raise issues under Article 8. The Geneva Convention does not contain any express provision entitling those recognised as refugees to family reunion but most Council of Europe states have provisions which facilitate some degree of family reunion for recognised refugees.

The establishment of "family life" is essentially a question of fact depending upon the reality of close personal ties.[314] A parent-child relationship where the child is born of a marriage will give rise to *de iure* family life which is only severed in exceptional circumstances. However, relationships which give rise to de facto family life are also brought within the protection of Article 8. The Court takes a pragmatic approach and will consider factors such as whether the couple lives together, the length of their relationship and whether they have demonstrated their commitment to each other by having children together

311 In 2003 the EU adopted Directive 2003/86/EC on the right to family reunification. Articles 9-12 of that directive expressly regulate the family reunification of refugees.

312 *Abdulaziz, Cabales and Balkandali v. the United Kingdom*, Applications Nos. 9214/80, 9473/81 and 9474/81, judgment of 28 May 1985.

313 *Moustaquim v. Belgium*, Application No. 12313/86, judgment of 18 February 1991.

314 *K. and T. v. Finland*, Application No. 25702/94, judgment of 12 July 2001.

or by any other means.[315] Thus the notion extends beyond mere blood ties[316] (which are insufficient in and of themselves) to other ties – whether financial or practical. However, the Court has distinguished between core and non-core family – between dependent family (children) and non-dependants (elderly parents) – "family life" could not be relied on in the latter.[317]

The notion of "family life" may be said to have a retrospective and prospective element – the Court adjudges whether it would be ended, maintained or affected in the future.[318] In contrast, Article 8 in the aspect of physical integrity tends to be based on prospective factors – whether a person's physical or mental state is so unstable that any deterioration caused by the implementation of a deportation decision might give rise to successful Convention claims.[319] Both must be substantiated. To establish "family life", applicants must be given a fair opportunity to present family claims in the absence of bad faith by the authorities;[320] or deceit perpetuated by the parties.[321]

Interference with the right to family life

Under Article 8 the Convention organs must first decide whether there has been an "interference" with the right to respect for family life. It is important to note that it is only respect for family life that is guaranteed under Article 8 and not choice of residence. If it is reasonable to expect the family unit to conduct their family life elsewhere there will be no interference (and thus no need to justify it). Clearly if individuals have been given international protection on the basis that they cannot safely return to their country of origin, it would seem axiomatic that it is not reasonable to expect them to conduct their family life in that state.

However, this has not always been the approach of the Court. *Gül v. Switzerland*[322] concerned a Turkish Kurd who sought asylum in Switzerland and was later joined by his badly injured epileptic wife who was granted a humanitarian residence permit. The couple sought permission for their older child, who had

---

315 *Al-Nashif v. Bulgaria*, Application No. 50963/99, judgment of 20 June 2002.

316 Ibid.

317 *Slivenko v. Latvia*, Application No. 48321/99, judgment of 9 October 2003.

318 *Lupsa v. Romania*, Application No. 10337/04, judgment of 8 June 2006.

319 See above, *Bensaid* and *Paramsothy*.

320 *Kamal v. the United Kingdom*, Application No. 8378/78, decision of 14 May 1980, 20 DR 168, and *Miah, Islam v. the United Kingdom*, Application No. 19546/92, decision of 13 March 1992.

321 See *Mubilanzila Mayeka and Kaniki Mitunga v. Belgium*, Application No. 13178/03, judgment of 12 October 2006.

322 Application No. 23218/94, judgment of 19 February 1996, paragraph 43.

been left behind in Turkey, to join them in Switzerland but were refused because although they were resident, they were not yet domiciled, in Switzerland. The matter was contested for many years. The parents' residence permits were renewed each year on the express basis that the wife could not return to Turkey. This is a similar situation to that of many granted subsidiary protection who are not recognised as Geneva Convention refugees.[323]

The Court found in *Gül* that the refusal to allow the child to join his parents did not constitute an interference under Article 8, paragraph 1 – and consequently there was no need to determine whether the interference was justified under Article 8, paragraph 2, despite the fact that the Swiss renewed the parents' residence permits each year on the basis that the mother could not return to Turkey. The Court noted: "It has not been proved that she could not later have received appropriate medical treatment in specialist hospitals in Turkey."[324] The Court also found that the father left Turkey of his own free will, "preferring"[325] to seek employment in Switzerland, although the evidence was that he had been required to abandon his asylum claim in order to accept the humanitarian permit which the Swiss authorities were offering. Furthermore, the Court considered that the older child had grown up in the "cultural and linguistic environment"[326] of Turkey (although the child was Kurdish, had lived with various Kurdish families, had never been to school in Turkey and did not speak Turkish). On the basis of the foregoing "facts", the Court held that there had been no interference with the right to respect for family life as it considered that there were no obstacles preventing the family from conducting their family life in Turkey. The Court did not, however, exclude the possibility of a violation of Article 8 in circumstances where it was established that family life could not be conducted in the state of origin. In a strongly worded dissenting opinion Judges Martens and Russo noted that the Court "remains free to make its own appreciation"[327] of the facts, but they warned of the danger of the Court taking into account "facts other than those which are properly established".[328]

---

323 The EU Directive 2001/55/EC on temporary protection provides at Article 15 for family reunion for those entitled to temporary protection. The EU Qualification Directive (Article 23) pays lip service to family unity for those entitled to international protection.

324 *Gül v. Switzerland*, op. cit., paragraph 41.

325 Ibid., dissenting opinion of Judge Martens, approved by Judge Russo, paragraph 3.

326 Ibid., paragraph 42.

327 Ibid., dissenting opinion, paragraph 3.

328 Ibid. The dissenting opinion further noted that, leaving the question of medical care on one side, the "choice" in question was between renouncing their son or their little daughter whose interests almost certainly would have required that she should be left behind.

In *Bulus v. Sweden*, the Commission declared admissible a case concerning Syrian adolescents threatened with expulsion when their mother and sister were permitted to remain.[329] However, in *Aksar v. the United Kingdom* the Commission declared inadmissible a complaint concerning the refusal to admit the extended family of a person with refugee status.[330] More recently a friendly settlement has been reached (and visas issued) in the case of *Osman* involving the siblings of a Somali granted international protection in the United Kingdom whose family was living in conditions of squalor in Kenya.[331]

Is the interference justified under Article 8, paragraph 2?

There are a number of prerequisites under Article 8, paragraph 2, in order to justify an interference with the right to respect for family life.

First, the restriction of the right must be carried out "in accordance with the law". The primary purpose of Article 8 is to guarantee that the state authorities afford the minimum degree of protection to applicants. The decision to expel an asylum seeker must have a "legal basis",[332] and the law in question must be of a certain quality – namely accessible, foreseeable and precise.[333]

Second, the interference with the right to "family life" must "pursue a legitimate aim", namely, in the interests of national security, public safety or the economic well-being of the country, for the prevention of crime or disorder.[334] The measure taken must be "necessary in a democratic society" and proportionate to the aim pursued. There is an imprecise boundary between positive and negative obligations but a fair balance must be struck between the interest of the individual and the interest of the community (*Gül*). States are also afforded a margin of appreciation in their decision-making procedures – it is suggested that this margin is widened in the context of nationality.[335]

---

329 35 DR 57.

330 *Askar v. the United Kingdom*, Application No. 26373/95, decision of 16 October 1995. Declared inadmissible.

331 *Osman and Others v. the United Kingdom*, Application No. 12698/06.

332 *Lupsa v. Romania*, Application No. 10337/04, judgment of 8 June 2006.

333 Ibid., paragraph 32.

334 See, for example, *Bensaid, Amrollahi v. Denmark* and *Sisojeva v. Latvia*, Application No. 60654/00, judgment of 16 June 2005. The remaining grounds are less prevalent in expulsion cases, for example the protection of health or morals, or for the protection of the rights and freedoms of others.

335 *Dalia v. France*, Application No. 26102/95, judgment of 19 February 1998, *Reports of judgments and decisions* 1998-I, p. 9, paragraph 52, and *Mehemi v. France*, judgment of 26 September 1997, *Reports* 1997-VI, p. 1971, paragraph 34.

"Integrated" aliens or long-term residents

The Grand Chamber of the Court in *Üner v. the Netherlands*[336] clarified the relative status of long-term residents to nationals:

> "Even if a non-national holds a very strong residence status and has attained a high degree of integration, his or her position cannot be equated with that of a national when it comes to the ... power of the Contracting States to expel aliens."[337]

Article 8 protects persons from arbitrary interference by state authorities and this applies "regardless of whether an alien entered the host country as an adult or at a very young age, or was perhaps even born there".[338] However, in the dissenting opinion of Judges Costa, Zupančič and Türmen, "foreign nationals – who, like Mr. Üner, have been residing legally in a country – should be granted the same fair treatment and a legal status as close as possible to that accorded to nationals."[339]

The fact-dependency of the Court decision making in these cases has been criticised as lacking legal certainty and creating a "lottery" for national authorities.[340]

Long-term residents – Family life and private life

The Court in *Üner* noted that the protection of Article 8 in its "private life" aspect also applies to integrated aliens.[341] Article 8 protects "the right to establish and develop relationships with other human beings and the outside world and can sometimes embrace aspects of an individual's social identity ...".[342] The concept of private life is constituted by a network of personal, social and economic relations or ties between the settled migrants and their community.[343]

---

336 Application No. 46410/99, judgment of 18 October 2006.

337 Ibid., citing *Moustaquim v. Belgium*, judgment of 18 May 1991, Series A No. 193, p. 20, paragraphs 49, 52 and 56.

338 Ibid., paragraph 55.

339 *Üner v. the Netherlands*, dissenting opinion, paragraph 5.

340 For example, Judge Morenilla dissenting in *Nasri v. France*, Application No. 19465/92, judgment of 13 July 1995; Judge Martens, dissenting in *Boughanemi v. France*, Application No. 22070/93, judgment of 24 April 1996, and Judges Costa and Tulkens dissenting in *Baghli v. France*. See also Reid, K., *A practitioner's guide to the European Convention on Human Rights*, London: Sweet & Maxwell, 1998, p. 383.

341 *Üner v.the Netherlands*, op. cit., paragraph 95, citing *Dalia v. France*, Application No. 26102/95, judgment of 19 February 1998, paragraphs 42-45. Moreover, the Court has recognised that Article 8 applies to the exclusion of displaced persons from their homes (see *Cyprus v. Turkey* (GC), Application No. 25781/94, judgment of 10 May 2001, paragraph 175.

342 *Üner v.the Netherlands*, op. cit.,, judgment, paragraph 59, citing *Mikulić v. Croatia*, Application No. 53176/99, judgment of 7 February 2002, paragraph 53.

343 *Üner v. the Netherlands*, op. cit., paragraph 69; and *Slievenko v. Latvia*, Application No. 48321/99, judgment of 9 October 2003.

The Court appeared to go one step further in the case of *Sisojeva and Others v. Latvia*.[344] The Chamber held that even if formal deportation orders had not actually been issued in respect of the applicants, the failure of the state authorities to regularise the applicant's immigration status after many years of being resident in Latvia constituted an interference with their private life. In the dissenting opinions of Judges Vaji and Briede, it was stated that the Convention does not create a right to a "particular type of residence permit".[345] The Grand Chamber of the Court on 15 January 2007 struck out the Article 8 claim as the matter giving rise to the claim was held to be "resolved" – the Latvian authorities had provided adequate options to regularise the applicants' status.

3. Children and asylum

Children refused protection may face a "real risk" of ill-treatment contrary to Articles 3 or 8 and particular suffering may be inflicted by virtue of their age and vulnerability. For children, as with adults, the threshold of severity under Article 3 remains high. The provisions of the UN Convention on the Rights of the Child are of key importance under Article 53 of the ECHR.

"Unaccompanied children"

Refugee and migrant children may be classed as being "among the world's most vulnerable populations" and face "particular risk when … separated from their parents and carers".[346] In particular, the phenomenon of separated or "unaccompanied" children is a challenge facing all member states. Unaccompanied children are arriving in member states for an array of reasons including trafficking for economic or sexual exploitation, fleeing from persecutors and war zones, or even family members or associates.[347] There is no consensus between the member states on how to deal with the situation but European and global initiatives stress the importance of adequate reception and care for an expelled child in their country of origin and that the "best interests of the child"[348] should guide a choice between repatriation and

---

344 Application No. 60654/00, judgment of 16 June 2005.

345 Ibid., dissenting opinion of Judges Vajić and Briede, paragraph 1.

346 "Human Rights Watch World Report 2002: children's rights". Accessible from www.hrw.org/wr2k2/children.html

347 See Babha, J. and Finch, N., "Seeking asylum alone", www.gardencourtchambers.co.uk/ news/news_detail.cfm?iNewsID=281.
See also the Save the Children Separated Children in Europe Programme, "Save the Children response to the 'Green Paper on a Community return policy on illegal immigrants'", COM(2002)175. Accessible from:http://ec.europa.eu/justice_home/news/ consulting_public/return_policy/save_children_en.pdf

348 United Nations Convention on the Rights of the Child, 1989, Article 3, ratified by all EU member states and candidate countries.

removal.[349] These principles have been incorporated within the European Court's jurisprudence – impliedly *(Nsona)*[350] and explicitly *(Üner)*.[351] The Court is yet to develop a set of principles relating to child-specific forms and manifestations of persecution as required by the United Nations Convention on the Rights of the Child.[352]

Two further problems specifically affect child asylum seekers. First, there may be an absence of or inadequate legal representation for child asylum seekers.[353] The second problem relates to the inability of domestic courts to place children in an appropriate legal framework.[354] However, this also poses a problem for the Convention organs – are the legal principles developed in relation to adult asylum seekers satisfactorily applied to child asylum seekers, in view of their age and vulnerability?

Children and Article 3

In general, the Court has exercised a high degree of scrutiny over the positive obligations of states to protect children from the type of treatment prohibited by Article 3.[355] Specifically in the context of the need for international protection, Article 3 claims rest upon the kind of factual matrix considered above, but take age and vulnerability into account. The Court in *Mubilanzila Mayeka and Kaniki Mitunga v. Belgium*[356] noted that the child's position was characterised by her very young age; the vulnerable position in which she was placed (which resulted in considerable distress); and the circumstances of her deportation, which would have caused her extreme anxiety. Leaving this 5 year-old girl in an adult detention centre pending deportation and failing to take steps for the child to receive childcare during and after the deportation displayed a complete lack of humanity towards a child of her age and situation and, as such, amounted to inhuman treatment within Article 3. It was further noted that there were other practical alternatives which were not utilised but would have been more beneficial for the higher interest of the child, as protected in the 1989 United Nations Convention on the Rights of the Child.

---

349 Council Resolution of 26 June 1997 on unaccompanied minors who are nationals of third countries (97/C 221/03). Official Journal C 221, 19 July 1997, Article 5(1-2).

350 *Nsona v. the Netherlands*, decision of 28 November 1996, RJD 1996-VI, No. 23.

351 *Üner v. the Netherlands*, Application No. 46410/99, judgment of 18 October 2006.

352 UNCRC General Comment No. 6, 2005.

353 "Seeking asylum alone".

354 Ibid.

355 See *Aydin v. Turkey*, Application No. 23178/94, judgment of 28 June 1997; *Z and Others v. the United Kingdom*, Application No. 29392/95, judgment of 10 May 2001.

356 Application No. 13178/03, judgment of 12 October 2006.

For the purposes of Article 3 a child must suffer extreme hardship or, it seems, a complete absence of childcare. Disease-ridden, unsanitary environments, lack of schooling and inability to communicate due to a language barrier would breach Article 3 (*Fadele v. the United Kingdom*).[357] Less favourable conditions such as a lower level of schooling or loss of benefits, having to leave the child in care, or accept the wardship of Court[358] or functionally present care[359] will not meet the Article 3 threshold.[360] The complete absence of childcare (*Taspinar v. the Netherlands*) or the fact that a boy lived on the run for two years in order to avoid expulsion to Syria (*Bulus v. Sweden*)[361] were situations falling within the ambit of Article 3. In sum, there must be real and practical obstacles.[362]

For children, as with adults,[363] an alleged deterioration in mental or physical health must be exceptional to fall within Article 3.[364] Where an applicant fails to establish that the same medical treatment is unavailable in the receiving state,[365] or the standard of health care is simply less favourable, but neverthe-less available, the ill-treatment complained of will not meet the Article 3 threshold and it is questionable whether it would meet that of Article 8.[366] Even where the Court accepts the seriousness of a physical condition, it will not necessarily give rise to a violation – for example the possible lack of medical treatment for a 3 year-old child with a debilitating hand condition was not regarded as being "life-threatening" or as having "life-incapacitating" effect and hence fell short of treatment prohibited by Article 3.[367] Similarly, a 5 year-old boy with Down's syndrome was not considered to be in a condition akin to "the final stages of a fatal illness".[368] This logic clearly underpinned the

---

357 Application No. 13078/87, judgment of 4 July 1991.

358 Application No. 11026/84, judgment of 9 October 1985, 44 DR 262.

359 Application No. 23366/94, judgment of 28 November 1996. Here arrangements were made by Swissair to meet the child at the airport and the Dutch authorities sent the child to live with the business relation of her father's sister – there being no living relatives.

360 Application No. 22471/93, judgment of 6 September 1994.

361 Application No. 9330/81, judgment of 19 January 1984, 35 DR 35 and (Rep) 39 DR 75.

362 Ibid.

363 For more information see above at page 59.

364 *D. v. the United Kingdom* (1997), 24 EHRR 423.

365 *Ovdienko v. Finland*, Application No. 1383/04, decision of 21 May 2005.

366 *Hukić v. Sweden*, Application No. 17416/05, decision of 27 September 2005, paragraph 3.

367 *Sorabjee v. the United Kingdom*, Application No. 23938/94, decision of 23 October 1995 (inadmissible).

368 *Hukić v. Sweden*, Application No. 17416/05, decision of 27 September 2005, paragraph 2.

decision in *P.P. and Others v. the United Kingdom*, where the risk of deterioration in psychological and physical health due to a change in environment reached neither the high threshold of Article 3 nor the lower standard of Article 8.

Children and Article 8

The Convention does not provide a right to choose where to live – the protection afforded to asylum seekers by Article 8 only exists where no practical alternatives exist. In cases of family reunification, where children apply to join family members in a member state the Court considers factors such as the child's linguistic and cultural links to his/her country of origin; whether he/she had been brought up by relatives and lived at a distance from his/her family for some time; and whether his/her family freely chose to leave their child in the country of origin. It is not enough that the parents prefer to develop family life with their children in a member state as opposed to their country of origin.[369] It appears that it must be considered reasonable for parents to be expected to return to their country of origin.[370]

The Court adopted an almost utilitarian approach to family life in *Sen v. the Netherlands*[371] – it held that it was more favourable for one family member to be granted entry clearance to join four rather than for four to be removed to join one. It seems that Article 8 may not be relied on where children reach an age where they no longer require the degree of care expected by young children but are increasingly able to fend for themselves. *Tuquabo-Tekle and Others v. the Netherlands*[372] was factually similar to *Sen*, save for the age of the children left in the state of origin – 15 (*Tuquabo-Tekle*) instead of 9 (*Sen*). The child was "after all, still a minor", providing no justificatory element to adjudge the case differently from that of *Sen*.[373] The recent case of *Osman and Others v. the United Kingdom*[374] concerned the family of a Somali granted international protection in the United Kingdom. The family had fled to Kenya and were living in appalling conditions of abject poverty there. They were refused permission to join the parent in the United Kingdom. All appeals were unsuccessful and the government maintained its refusal. However, once the case was communicated to the United Kingdom Government by the European Court, the government agreed to issue the necessary visas.

---

369 *Ahmut v. the Netherlands*, Application No. 21702/93, decision of 12 October 1994.

370 *Tuquabo-Tekle and Others v. the Netherlands*, Application No. 60665/00, judgment of 1 December 2005, paragraph 49. See also *Benamar v. the Netherlands*, Application No. 43786/04, decision of 5 April 2005; *I.M. v. the Netherlands*, Application No. 41266/98, decision of 25 March 2003; and *Chandra and Others v. the Netherlands*, Application No. 53102/99, decision of 13 May 2003.

371 Application No. 31465/96, judgment of 21 December 2001.

372 Application No. 60665/00, judgment of 1 December 2005.

373 Ibid., paragraph 51.

374 Application No. 12698/06. Friendly settlement reached.

Where a parent or custodian is not granted asylum, their exclusion may well subject their children to ill-treatment of the kind prohibited by Article 8. This may also be incompatible with global standards in relation to the "best interests" of a child – in particular those under the United Nations Convention on the Rights of the Child.[375] Nevertheless, the jurisprudence of the Court suggests that in the case of very young children they may be of an adaptable age to cope even with "wholly inadequate" health and educational environments within the receiving state.[376] The analysis is slightly different where a non-national parent faces expulsion and the children are in the custody of a parent with citizenship or residence rights, after a divorce or separation. The Court appears to place more emphasis on the personal links to the child in such cases rather than the personal links to the territory.[377]

Access to the European Court of Human Rights (see below) is also available to very young children even if there is no parent able to bring the case on their behalf. The Court's jurisprudence makes it clear that complaints under the Convention may be brought before the Court on a child's behalf – for example by an NGO or a lawyer where the children are not in a position to do so themselves, or their parents cannot act. The Court will ensure that they are not prevented from bringing their complaint for such reasons.[378]

4. Status of those whose claim is being examined or has been rejected

Status and related issues

Whilst the prime concern of those seeking international protection is not to be returned to a situation where they will be at risk of prohibited treatment, recent years have seen a sharp increase in a number of issues surrounding the situation in which they find themselves even though there is no immediate

---

375 Judges Costa, Zupančič and Türmen in *Üner* (dissenting), at paragraphs 5-7, citing the conclusions of the Presidency of the Tampere European Council on 15 and 16 October 1999; the Seville European Council of 21 and 22 June 2002; the Council of Europe Committee of Ministers Recommendation Rec(2000)15 at paragraphs 36-38; the Parliamentary Assembly Recommendation 1504 (2000) and Committee of Ministers Recommendation Rec(2002)4. At a global level they cited the 1989 United Nations Convention on the Rights of the Child.

376 *Fadele v. the United Kingdom,* Application No. 13078/87, decision of 12 February 1990.

377 See *Berrehab v. the Netherlands,* Application No. 10730/84, judgment of 21 June 1988.

378 See *Scozzari and Giunta v. Italy.* Applications Nos. 39221/98 and 41963/98, judgment of 13 July 2000, and *P., C. and S. v. the United Kingdom,* Application No. 56547/00, judgment of 16 July 2002, *Covezzi and Morselli v. Italy,* Application No. 52763/99, judgment of 9 May 2003. Also see Mole, N., "Litigating children's rights affected by armed conflict before the European Court of Human Rights", pp. 167-81, in Arts, K. and Popovski, V. (eds.), *International criminal accountability and the rights of children*, Cambridge, Cambridge University Press.

threat of return. Status and the associated documents evidencing status are issues falling within the private life rubric of Article 8 (see *Smirnova v. Russia*[379] *Sisojeva v. Latvia* below).

The situation of those seeking international protection

For those claiming asylum within the EU, the Reception Conditions Directive stipulates (Article 6) that everyone who lodges an application for asylum must be given within three days a document testifying that he or she is allowed to stay in the territory of the member state whilst the asylum claim is being examined.

The situation of those recognised as in need of international protection

Those who are recognised as refugees under the Geneva Convention will be granted that status and all the benefits that flow from it. Within the EU those who are recognised under the Qualification Directive as needing subsidiary protection must also be granted both residence permits and the other benefits conferred by Chapter VII of the directive.

Those who are outside the EU, or who fall outside the scope of the Geneva Convention or the directive and are protected from return only by the ECHR, remain subject to whatever provisions national law has made for them.

The situation of those refused international protection

Since the criteria under the Geneva Convention, EU law and the ECHR, for being granted international protection from return are very stringent, very few of those who apply are granted it. However, even if there is no legal impediment to their return, in many member states significant numbers of those refused both kinds of international protection cannot be returned to their country of origin for various reasons: their citizenship is uncertain; they lack the necessary documentation and often the host states have no resident diplomatic presence from the country of origin; the transportation costs of returning them to their country of origin are prohibitive; or the host states lack the resources (or the will) to locate and remove them.

In both sets of circumstances people in many states find themselves in some kind of legal limbo, with uncertain status and more importantly no proper documentation setting out their position. Their entitlement to seek employment, to housing, to welfare benefits, to education and to health care is also precarious. Amnesty International states that such abject poverty is undignified and blocks "all avenues to a normal life". Amnesty believes further that rejected asylum seekers are forced into destitution in order to compel their return home.[380]

---

379 Applications Nos. 46133/99 and 48183/99, judgment of 24 July 2003.

380 See Amnesty Action Campaign, "UK: the road to destitution for rejected asylum seekers". Available at: www.amnesty.org.uk/actions_details.asp?ActionID=226.

The approach taken by the ECtHR to status and documentation

Article 8 ECHR also governs the status (in relation to the right to residence documents, access to welfare and health care, and employment) of those who cannot be expelled. A separate opinion annexed to the Commission's report in *H.L.R. v. France* is on this point. Mr Cabral Barreto (now the Portuguese judge in the Court) considered that a finding by the Strasbourg organs that an expulsion would constitute a violation of Article 3 of the ECHR implied not only that no expulsion should take place but also that any extant expulsion order must be cancelled. He also considered that if a breach of Article 8 of the ECHR were to be avoided, some kind of residence permit must be granted which would allow the individual access to employment and the social welfare system.[381] The point was not expressly taken up by the Court in *B.B. v. France*[382] where the Court considered that the complaint could be struck off once the threat of immediate expulsion had been lifted even though this meant that a very sick man was left in an uncertain status requiring "safe conduct" to attend hospital appointments and reporting at regular intervals to the gendarmerie and the police. In *Ahmed v. Austria*,[383] the Court had found that it would be a violation of the Convention to expel the applicant to Somalia, but had no jurisdiction to rule on whether or not he had been rightfully stripped of his status as a refugee under the Geneva Convention. His entitlement to social, medical and welfare benefits was dependent on his refugee status. Ironically and tragically, although prevented from being expelled to Somalia by the ruling of the European Court, he was left in such isolation and destitution as a result of the loss of refugee status that he committed suicide some months later. The Court has frequently stated that Article 8 does not normally go as far as guaranteeing an individual the right to a particular kind of residence permit so long as the solution proposed by the authorities permits him to enjoy his right to respect for family and private life – see, for example, *Dremlyuga v. Latvia*.[384]

However, in some situations a particular permit may be required. For those who are entitled to subsidiary protection (and thus to a residence permit) under the Qualification Directive, the case of *Aristimuno Mendizabal v. France* is relevant.[385] The case concerned the repeated issue of temporary permits but also the failure to issue the long-term permit to which the applicant was entitled. The Court examined the compatibility with Article 8 of the Convention of the failure of the French authorities to grant a long-term residence permit to a person who had a right to reside in France under both EU law and certain

---

381 Separate opinion of Mr Cabral Barreto, *H.L.R. v. France*, Application No. 24573/94, report of 7 December 1995.

382 Application No. 30930/96, judgment of 7 September 1998.

383 Application No. 25964/94, judgment of 7 December 1996.

384 Application No. 66729/01, decision of 29 April 2003.

385 Application No. 51431/99, judgment of 17 January 2006.

provisions of French domestic law. Focusing on the EU law aspects of the case, they found that the interference with the applicant's right to respect for private (and family) life, occasioned by the failure to issue the requisite long-term residence permit, was not in accordance with the law – both EU and national law – and that it was therefore unnecessary to determine whether it would otherwise have been justified. The Qualification Directive requires states to issue those entitled to subsidiary protection with residence permits. The Court in *Aristimuno* found no violation of Article 13 (the right to an effective remedy), and in awarding the applicant 50 000 euros compensation for the violation of Article 8 made no mention of the right to compensation which she had as a matter of EU law for the failure of the French authorities to give proper effect to the directive.[386]

The case of *Sisojeva v. Latvia* is instructive for many of those whose need for international protection has not been recognised but who are not being removed.[387] It concerned a family of ethnic Russians whose presence in Latvia remained unregularised although the authorities were not taking active steps to remove them. The Chamber of the Court found that there were positive obligations under Article 8 which had not been observed:

> "It is not enough for the host state to refrain from deporting the person concerned; it must also by means of positive measures if necessary, afford him or her the opportunity to exercise the rights in question without interference."

The case was referred to the Grand Chamber and decided by it on 15 January 2007. The Chamber had concluded that the prolonged failure to regularise the applicants' status constituted a violation of Article 8; the Grand Chamber struck out this claim because the situation has now been "resolved" by the Latvian authorities.

It should be noted in this respect that other breaches of Convention rights are routinely adjudicated upon by the Court in relation to the past conduct of the authorities. For example, breaches of Article 5 are regularly found long after the detainee has been released. Breaches of Article 8 are frequently found long after an unjustified interference by the state authorities with family life. However, in immigration cases such as *Sisojeva*, the Grand Chamber did not consider it necessary to adjudicate on alleged past violations of the right to private life under Article 8. The applicants had applied without success for residence permits over a prolonged period of time but only when the case was before the Grand Chamber did the state recognise that it had a duty to regularise their situation. Thus the Court did not find it necessary to rule on the past violations of their rights.[388]

---

386 See decision of the ECJ in *Francovich and Bonifaci v. Italy* (Cases C-6 and 9/90) [1991] ECR I-5357.

387 Application No. 60654/00, Chamber judgment of 16 June 2006, Grand Chamber judgment of 15 January 2007.

388 *Sisojeva and Others v. Latvia*, Application No. 60654/00, judgment (GC) of 15 January 2007. See especially paragraph 94.

The mere absence of proper documentation may in itself constitute a violation. In *Smirnova v. Russia*[389] the Court considered a complaint relating to the confiscation of the applicant's internal passport which left her without an identity document. The Court found that the interference with her Article 8 rights flowed "not from an instantaneous act, but from a number of everyday inconveniences". It found that in their everyday life Russian citizens have to prove their identity unusually often such as when buying train tickets or changing money and that the internal passport was required for more crucial needs such as finding employment or receiving medical care. "The deprivation of a passport therefore represented a continuing interference with the applicant's private life."[390]

As with the right to a residence permit, the Qualification Directive obliges EU states to provide those entitled to refugee status or subsidiary protection with specified access to employment, accommodation, health care, education and social welfare. Any interference with either the positive or negative obligations contained in Article 8 of the ECHR, protected rights in states where the Qualification Directive applies, will automatically violate the Convention, as not being in accordance with the law. As a matter of EU law it will found an action in damages.

Although there is no right to a home to be found in the Convention – Article 8 only provides for respect for the home which one already has – it is arguable that the right to life (Article 2), the prohibition on degrading treatment under Article 3, or the right to "moral and physical integrity" under the private life rubric of Article 8 would prohibit a state from leaving anyone within its jurisdiction in conditions of complete destitution in the same way that expulsion to face destitution was found to violate Article 3 in *D. v. the United Kingdom*. In *O'Rourke v. the United Kingdom*[391] the Court declared the case inadmissible because it found that the applicant had brought his homelessness upon himself, but the Court did not exclude the possibility that his Convention rights could have been engaged had the state been responsible for his plight.[392]

The same principles apply to Article 1 of Protocol No. 1 (the peaceful enjoyment of possessions). The Court has looked at the entitlement of foreigners to social assistance under Article 1 of Protocol No. 1 in a number of cases. It considers that the right to emergency assistance is a pecuniary right falling within the ambit of that provision without the need for it to be linked to the payment of

---

389 Applications Nos. 46133/99 and 48183/99, judgment of 24 July 2003.

390 Ibid., paragraph 97.

391 Application No. 39022/97, decision of 26 June 2001.

392 For a detailed examination of the Convention rights at issue for destitute asylum seekers see the judgment of the United Kingdom House of Lords in the case of *Limbuela and Others* [2005] UKHL 66, 3 November 2005.

taxes and other contributions. In *Gaygusuz v. Austria*[393] and *Koua Poirrez v. France*[394] the Court found that the denial of access to welfare benefits, to which the applicants would otherwise have been entitled, simply because they were foreigners, violated that article taken together with Article 14 which prohibits discrimination. The Qualification Directive's provisions on welfare benefits are also relevant for EU states.

A central issue, over which western European states adopt differing positions, concerns the questions as to whether asylum seekers awaiting consideration of their claim should be obliged to work, should be permitted to work, or denied a work permit. In earlier years, some states required asylum seekers to undertake "community work", raising the question as to whether such work was effectively "forced or compulsory labour" as defined by the International Labour Organization,[395] and thus raising issues under Article 4 of the ECHR. The separate opinion in the report in *H.L.R. v. France* expressed the view that the refusal to accord the means of subsistence to a person whose expulsion had been ruled to be in violation of the Convention raised issues under Article 8 of the ECHR.[396] The same must apply to those who cannot be expelled whilst their applications to remain are being determined. For EU states the Reception Conditions Directive applies and gives those who have duly applied for asylum enforceable rights.

It should also be noted that fewer and fewer asylum seekers are now formally recognised as convention refugees. Instead they tend to be given exceptional leave to remain (in the United Kingdom), or are otherwise permitted to remain

---

393 Application No. 17371/90, judgment of 16 September 1996.

394 Application No. 40892/98, judgment of 30 September 2003.

395 For instance, in the *Iversen* case a majority of the Commission concluded: "The concept of compulsory or forced labour cannot be understood solely in terms of the literal meaning of the words, and has in fact come to be regarded in international law and practice, as evidenced in part by the provisions and application of the ILO conventions and resolutions on forced labour, as having certain elements ... these elements of forced or compulsory labour are, first, that the work or service is performed by the worker against his will and, secondly, that the requirement that the work or service be performed is unjust or oppressive or the work or service itself involves avoidable hardship" (*Iversen v. Norway*, Application No. 1468/62, *Yearbook* 6 (1963) 278, p. 328). The Commission appears to take the view that service is capable of constituting "forced or compulsory labour" within the meaning of the Convention, even when it has been undertaken by the consent of a person who was in fact incapable of exercising a free choice (*W, X, Y and Z v. the United Kingdom*, Applications Nos. 3435, 3436, 3437 and 3438/67, XI *Yearbook* (1968) 562, p. 594). The Court has further added that remunerated work may also qualify as forced or compulsory labour and a lack of remuneration and of reimbursement of expenses may constitute a relevant factor in considering what is proportionate (*Van der Mussele* case, judgment of 27 November 1983, Series A, No. 70).

396 Separate opinion of Mr Cabral Barreto, report of the Commission in *H.L.R. v. France*, Application No. 24573/94, report of 7 December 1995.

temporarily on humanitarian grounds. Such de facto refugees are more susceptible to arbitrary decisions by competent authorities and do not automatically
enjoy the same rights as "Convention refugees". These rights are spelt out in
the Geneva Convention and include, for instance, the right to public relief and
assistance, and the right to engage in wage-earning employment. Other organs
of the Council of Europe have sought to improve the condition of de facto refugees.
In particular, Recommendation No. R (84) 1 of the Committee of Ministers
reaffirms that the principle of *non-refoulement* applies to both convention and
de facto refugees.[397] The European Convention on Human Rights, however,
does not include any right to work,[398] so any complaint made on that basis
would be inadmissible *ratione materiae*. For EU states the Reception Conditions
Directive applies.

5. Non-discrimination: Article 14 and Protocol No. 12

Article 14 of the European Convention on Human Rights prohibits discrimination on the grounds of "sex, race, colour, language, religion, political or other
opinion, national or social origin, association with a national minority, property,
birth or other status".

Article 14 is not a free-standing right and the protection from discrimination
may only be invoked in relation to the enjoyment of other Convention rights.
There must be a difference in treatment which falls within the ambit of another
Convention right[399] irrespective of the level of severity of the discrimination
suffered. (There need not necessarily be a breach of a Convention right).[400]
Furthermore, the state must show a reasonable and objective justification for
the treatment – that it pursued a legitimate aim and was proportionate to that
aim.[401]

The Court's jurisprudence under Article 14 specifically in the context of asylum
is sparse. However, complaints are usually made in relation to distinctions based
on nationality in relation to certain entitlements or benefits.[402] The Court has

---

397 Committee of Ministers, 25 January 1984.

398 See, for example, *Neigel v. France*, Application No. 18725/91, judgment of 17 March 1997.

399 See, for example, *Gaygusuz v. Austria*, Application No. 17371/90, judgment of 16
     September 1996, paragraph 36.

400 See, for example, *Botta v. Italy*, Application No. 21439/93, judgment of 24 February
     1998; and *Van der Mussele v. Belgium*, Application No. 8919/80, Series A, No. 70,
     judgment of 23 November 1983.

401 *Abdulaziz, Cabales and Balkandali v. the United Kingdom*, judgment of 28 May 1985,
     Series A, No. 94, paragraph 72.

402 Explanatory Report on Protocol No. 12 to the ECHR, paragraph 19. Accessed from:
     www.humanrights.coe.int/Prot12/Protocol%2012%20and%20Exp%20Rep.htm

declared inadmissible a complaint under Article 14 taken together with Article 6, concerning the failure of the state to provide, in domestic law, a right to appeal against the decision of a regional court refusing refugee status.[403] The Commission has also declared inadmissible a claim under Article 14 read together with Article 3 as to whether the state must provide, as a matter of domestic law, a declaratory decision as to whether the applicant is thought to be endangered within the meaning of Article 33, paragraph 1, of the Geneva Convention – the Article 3 claim was unsubstantiated.[404] The recent case of *Saadi v. the United Kingdom* did not consider whether a list of nationalities compiled in respect of detention in the United Kingdom was discriminatory under Article 14.[405] This case has been referred to the Grand Chamber.

Proposals to increase the guarantee to equality and non-discrimination date back to the 1960s and in recent years, the European Commission against Racism and Intolerance (ECRI), the Steering Committee for Equality between Women and Men (CDEG) and the Steering Committee for Human Rights (CDDH) have taken steps to reinforce the protection afforded under the ECHR in these areas. Protocol No. 12 creates a free-standing equality right. Article 1 states:

> "The enjoyment of any right set forth by law shall be secured without discrimination on any ground such as sex, race, colour, language, religion, political or other opinion, national or social origin, association with a national minority, property, birth or other status."

"Any right set forth by law" primarily refers to national law, but in EU states will also refer to the relevant EU regulations and directives.[406] The new protection is thus similar to that of Article 26 of the ICCPR.[407]

The International Convention on the Elimination of All Forms of Racial Discrimination (CERD) is also relevant in the context of non-discrimination and asylum. CERD specifically prohibits discrimination on the grounds of "race, colour, descent, or national or ethnic origin" and applies to distinction and exclusion. The convention is built around the principle stated in the preamble to the Universal Declaration of Human Rights: "all human beings are born free and equal in dignity and rights".

---

403 *S.N. v. the Netherlands*, Application No. 38088/97, decision of 4 May 1999.

404 *Hasan Gundogdnu v. Austria*, Application No. 33052/96, decision of 6 March 1997.

405 Application No. 13229/03, judgment of 11 July 2006.

406 Protocol No. 12 opened for signature in November 2000, and entered into force on 1 April 2005, upon being ratified by 10 states. As at 14 December 2006, 14 member states have both signed and ratified, 24 have signed but not ratified, and 11 have neither signed nor ratified.

407 Explanatory Report on Protocol No. 12 to the ECHR, paragraph 19.

6. Article 16 – Restrictions on the political activity of aliens

Article 16 states: "Nothing in Articles 10, 11 and 14 shall be regarded as preventing the High Contracting Parties from imposing restrictions on the political activities of aliens."[408]

There has been very little jurisprudence of either the Commission or Court on this article and as long ago as 1977 the Parliamentary Assembly of the Council of Europe (PACE) recommended its deletion from the Convention[409] and continues to champion the repeal of Article 16 today with reference to other Convention protections. First, Article 1 clearly guarantees rights to all persons within a state's jurisdiction, and Article 14 underlines the importance of non-discrimination. Second, states could continue to legitimately restrict the political rights of foreigners under Articles 10 and 11. PACE has stated that the repeal of Article 16:

> "would furthermore be perfectly in line with the aim of the [Council of Europe] to achieve 'further progress in building a Europe without dividing lines ... to be based on the common values embodied in the Statute of the Council of Europe: democracy, human rights, the rule of law', in the terms of the Warsaw Declaration".[410]

The Court had the opportunity to consider its scope in the case of *Piermont v. France*,[411] which concerned the rights of a German MEP in a French territory. The Court held that the French Government could not rely on Article 16 as the applicant was not only a European Union citizen but also an MEP, and the relevant territory participated in the European elections. Since the ruling of the Court in *Chahal* that a person cannot be expelled to face risk of treatment contrary to Article 3 even if he is allegedly a threat to national security, governments may try to rely on the provisions of Article 16 in the future. It will of course be for the Strasbourg organs to define the content of the phrase "political activities". It has been suggested that a narrow interpretation might well be taken which would include only matters directly part of the political process such as the setting up and operating of political parties or participation

---

408 Article 10 relates to freedom of expression, Article 11 to freedom of association and assembly, and Article 14 to non-discrimination in the enjoyment of Convention rights.

409 Recommendation 799 (1977) on the political rights of aliens, Council of Europe Parliamentary Assembly, 28th Ordinary Session.

410 Report of the Parliamentary Assembly of the Council of Europe at the 943rd meeting, 19 October 2005. CM/Monitor(2005)1, Volume, 11 October 2005, paragraphs 35-39. Accessed from: https://wcd.coe.int/ViewDoc.jsp?BackColorInternet=9999CC&BackColorIntranet=FFBB55&BackColorLogged=FFAC75&id=903339#P260_29169

411 Applications Nos. 15773/89 and 15774/89, judgment of 27 April 1995.

in elections.[412] At the Funchal Colloquy, Mr Frowein suggested that it could not be discounted that the Commission and Court would consider that the principle of proportionality, inasmuch as it applies to the provisions of the Convention in general, should also be applied to Article 16.[413] The importance of Article 53 should be remembered in this context. Articles 10, 11 and 14 all have corresponding provisions in the International Covenant on Civil and Political Rights (Articles 19, 21, 22 and 26) but the Covenant has no provision corresponding to Article 16.[414] Furthermore, there is no corresponding clause in the IACHR or the ACHPR. The Parliamentary Assembly of the Council of Europe has stated therefore that the ECHR stands alone in restricting the political activities of aliens and this restriction dates from a time, prior to the entry into force of the above-mentioned treaties, when it was considered legitimate to restrict the rights of foreigners generally.

7. Racism, xenophobia and the media

In the past decades the media have been increasingly responsible for encouraging the public to adopt and develop negative attitudes towards asylum seekers, frequently labelling as "bogus" all those who are not eventually admitted to the very exclusive category of Geneva Convention refugees. This has had a significant impact on the lives of asylum seekers, refugees and migrants in terms of their ability to integrate within communities and in terms of social acceptance.

There have been a number of important steps taken at a European level to combat racism and intolerance, in recognition of this increasingly serious phenomenon. The Parliamentary Assembly of the Council of Europe (PACE) in Recommendation 1277 (1995) on migrants, ethnic minorities and the media has expressed concern about the portrayal of such groups in the media. Furthermore, the Committee of Ministers has adopted Recommendation No. R (97) 20 on "hate speech" and No. R (97) 21 on the media and the promotion of a culture of tolerance. In a recent report on "The image of asylum seekers, migrants and refugees in the media", the PACE recommended that the Council of Europe invite the Steering Committee on the Media and New Communication Services (CDCM) to investigate the procedural protections and mechanisms for redress available to asylum seekers in the member states.[415]

---

412 See, for example, Harris, O'Boyle and Warbrick, *Law of the European Convention on Human Rights*, Butterworths, 1995.

413 *Proceedings of the Funchal-Colloquy*, Council of Europe, 1985, quoted in *La Convention Européenne des Droits de l'Homme*, Pettit, Decaux, Imbert, Economica, 1995.

414 Some parties to the ICCPR have entered reservations or declarations to the relevant articles of the covenant.

415 Report, Doc. 11011, 10 July 2006, "The image of asylum seekers, migrants and refugees in the media", Committee on Migration, Refugees and Population, rapporteur: Mrs Tana de Zulueta, Italy, Socialist Group, paragraphs 8.53-8.54. Accessed from http://assembly.coe.int/Mainf.asp?link=/Documents/WorkingDocs/Doc06/EDOC11011.htm

The European Commission has also proposed a framework decision on combating racism and xenophobia. It includes proposals to criminalise conduct carried out with a racist or xenophobic purpose – however, there is at present a lack of consensus regarding the mechanisms needed to achieve this.[416] The Committee on Migration has stated that the lack of agreement indicates that:

> "[w]hile there is agreement between member states that racism and xenophobia go against the fundamental values of Europe, the failure to agree a text is an indication that there are different ideas in Europe about freedom of expression and its boundaries".[417]

There are also independent human rights monitoring bodies in this field, including the European Commission against Racism and Intolerance (ECRI), which is committed to combating racism, xenophobia, anti-Semitism and intolerance. ECRI's remit includes the prevention of violence stemming from discrimination and prejudice on grounds of race, colour, language, religion, nationality and national or ethnic origin. ECRI fulfils a reporting function and aims to encourage dialogue with the media and identify viable solutions. The Framework Convention for the Protection of National Minorities also includes a monitoring mechanism requiring state parties to report to an Advisory Committee on measures taken to promote integration of asylum seekers within member states.

Governments have tended to find it in their interest not to discourage the negative portrayal of asylum seekers in the media. At the beginning of the 1990s the Danish Government took action against a journalist who had made a television programme about racism. The journalist took his case to Strasbourg. In the case of *Jersild v. Denmark*[418] the Court had to consider whether this television programme, which reported but did not criticise racist views, had been rightly sanctioned by the national authorities. The Court found a violation of Article 10 (the right to freedom of expression) because the film was a serious news programme and its presentation showed that it was not designed to be racist. A minority of the Court considered that the fight against racism was so fundamental to a democratic society that the journalist could have been required to make a more active criticism of racial discrimination without compromising his right to freedom of expression. It is important to note that in the *Jersild* case there was no suggestion that that journalist shared the racist views he was reporting.

The number of racial attacks in Europe including attacks on asylum seekers and their hostels is disturbing. "Islamophobia" has now emerged as a specific

---

416 Proposal for a Council framework decision on combating racism and xenophobia COM(2001)664.

417 Ibid., paragraph 31.

418 Application No. 15890/89, judgment of 23 September 1994.

form of racist attack – being manifested also in threats and harassment.[419] The media has played an increased role in the negative portrayal of Arabic peoples since 9/11 and often served to heighten fear and hostility towards Islam and Muslims. The furore over the publication of the Danish cartoons of the Islamic Prophet Muhammad was the subject of the decision in *Ben El Mahi*, which was declared inadmissible.[420] The European Court of Human Rights also declared inadmissible an Article 10 complaint by a British far-right extremist regarding the removal of a BNP poster from the window of his home. The poster connected British Muslims to the attack on the Twin Towers. The Court made its position explicit:

> "Such a general, vehement attack against a religious group, linking the group as a whole with a grave act of terrorism, is incompatible with the values proclaimed and guaranteed by the Convention, notably tolerance, social peace and non-discrimination."[421]

What obligations are incumbent on state parties under the ECHR? The positive duty under Article 1 to ensure that the Convention rights of everyone within the jurisdiction – including their right to life, to freedom from inhuman or degrading treatment, to moral and physical integrity and to the peaceful enjoyment of their possessions – is clearly engaged.[422] In relation to the protected rights of the asylum seekers the question posed by the European Court in *Osman*[423] arises. Did the state do everything that it could reasonably have been expected to do to protect an individual from harm of which it knew or ought to have known?

8. Terrorism

This little guide concludes with a few words on the present attempts[424] by governments to persuade the Court that diluting the protection guaranteed under Article 3 of the ECHR is a necessary response to terrorism. Terrorism is not a new phenomenon, and the claim of governments that respect for human rights

---

419 See Report of the European Union Monitoring Centre on Racism and Xenophobia (EUMC) on discrimination and Islamophobia in the EU available from: http://eumc. europa.eu/eumc/index.php?fuseaction=content.dsp_cat_content&catid=3fb38ad3 e22bb&contentid=4582d9f4345ad
See also report of 28 November 2006, available at: http://eumc.europa.eu/eumc/ index.php?fuseaction=content.dsp_cat_content&catid=4491243f59ed9.

420 *Ben El Mahi and Others v. Denmark*, Application No. 5853/06, decision of 11 December 2006.

421 *Norwood v. the United Kingdom*, Application No. 23131/03, decision of 16 November 2004.

422 See, for example, the judgment in *Ouranio Toxo v. Greece*, Application No. 74989/01, judgment of 20 October 2005.

423 *Osman v. the United Kingdom*, Application No. 23452/94, judgment of 28 October 1998.

424 *Ramzy v. the Netherlands*, Application No. 25424/05, case pending before the ECtHR.

must be sacrificed when states are targeted by terrorist acts is one which the Court has considered – and rejected – many times in the past fifty years. Terrorism itself is not a new issue in Europe, nor is it a new issue for the Convention organs. More than 350 cases involving state responses to the danger alleged to be posed by terrorists have been decided by the European institutions since the European Convention on Human Rights was adopted in 1950.[425]

Whilst empathising with the difficulties that terrorism poses for states, the approach of the Convention organs has been consistent: combating terrorism cannot justify violations of the very human rights which the terrorists are seeking to destroy, and in particular cannot be invoked to justify a dilution of the absolute prohibition on torture and inhuman and degrading treatment. Many of those who seek international protection are themselves fleeing from terrorism.

Security considerations have never been found by the Court to justify a dilution of the prohibition on torture and inhuman and degrading treatment even "in the most difficult circumstances, such as the fight against terrorism and organised crime".[426]

Although terrorist acts have been committed by those who are not citizens of any Council of Europe member state, some of the worst recent atrocities – including the London bombings on 7 July 2005 – have been the work of the affected state's own citizens. The clear duty under Article 1 of the ECHR, taken together with Articles 2 and 3 of the ECHR,[427] to protect the public from terrorism requires far more sophisticated methods and measures for dissuading disaffected young European Muslims from embracing an extremist position which leads them to resort to acts of extreme violence. The expulsion of non-national terrorist suspects to face absolutely prohibited treatment is not the solution to this very serious problem. Indeed, given the weakness of the procedural safeguards in place to ensure that the individuals concerned have been rightly identified as being terrorists, the suspicions may subsequently turn out to be unfounded and entirely innocent individuals may be subjected to torture. Such errors could even exacerbate the underlying problem.

The subject of asylum and terrorism is currently a hotbed of discussion.

---

425 See, for example, *Ireland v. the United Kingdom*, 1978, Series A, No. 25, 2 EHRR 25, *Tomasi v. France*, Application No. 12850/87, judgment of 27 August 1992, *Hugh Jordan v. the United Kingdom*, Application No. 24746/94, judgment of 4 May 2001, *Shamayev and Others v. Georgia and Russia*, Application No. 36378/02, judgment of 12 April 2005, *Öcalan v. Turkey*, Application No. 46221/99, judgment of 12 May 2005.

426 *Khashiyev and Akayeva v. Russia*, Applications Nos. 57942/00 and 57945/00, judgment of 24 February 2005, paragraph 17.

427 See, for example, *Mastromatteo v. Italy*, Application No. 377703/97, judgment of 24 October 2002.

Some national governments are attempting to dilute the absolute nature of the prohibition on expulsion to face treatment contrary to Article 3 as developed in the now voluminous body of Strasbourg case law. Only recently, in the case of *N. v. Finland*,[428] did the Court reiterate this tenet of European human rights law. Governments cannot escape their duties under the Convention by arguing that immigration control is a key attribute of their national sovereignty. While this is true, it cannot be used as a *carte blanche* to violate other principles of international law in general and the ECHR in particular. Nor can national governments trump the protection of the ECHR and escape their responsibilities by invoking Article 1F of the Geneva Convention. The Court has frequently noted that the protection offered by the ECHR is wider than that offered by the Geneva Convention, which applies only to a privileged group of persons who are protected from *refoulement* by virtue of the "convention reason" that puts them at risk.

The intervening governments in *Ramzy* also suggest that Article 3 of the Convention sets too low a threshold. This argument is difficult to sustain in the light of the particularly high threshold developed by the Court. For example, in *Vilvarajah and Others v. the United Kingdom*[429] the mere probability of ill-treatment was not enough. In *H.L.R. v. France*[430] the return of a member of a Colombian drugs cartel who had provided information which had led to a conviction and the imposition of lengthy sentences on his collaborators, to Colombia where the cartel was still active and powerful did not meet the threshold. In *Mamatkulov and Askarov v. Turkey*,[431] the Grand Chamber similarly found no violation of Article 3 in the return of Islamic fundamentalists to Uzbekistan.

Article 5 of the ECHR guarantees liberty and security of the person. The United Kingdom recently attempted to hold foreign nationals whom the government considered a threat to national security, but who could not be expelled because they would be at risk of treatment contrary to Article 3 of the ECHR in the countries to which they could be sent. The United Kingdom derogated from Article 5 of the ECHR under the provisions of Article 15 of the ECHR. The highest United Kingdom court (the House of Lords) rejected the validity of the derogation. The issue, and the United Kingdom Government's response to the judgment of the House of Lords, is now pending before the European Court.

On 11 July 2002 the Committee of Ministers of the Council of Europe adopted guidelines on human rights and the fight against terrorism.[432] Guideline XII deals with asylum, return (*refoulement*) and expulsion and is attached as an appendix to this text.

---

428 Application No. 38885/02, judgment of 26 July 2005.

429 Applications Nos. 13163/87, 13164/87 and 13165/87, judgment of 30 October 1991.

430 Application No. 24573/94, judgment of 29 April 1997.

431 Applications Nos. 46827/99 and 46951/99, judgment of 4 February 2005.

432 Guidelines on human rights and the fight against terrorism, adopted by the Committee of Ministers on 11 July 2002 at the 804th meeting of the Ministers' Deputies.

CIA rendition and secret prisons: a global "spider's web"

On 7 June 2006 PACE member Dick Marty, special rapporteur, presented his report (the Marty Report) into alleged secret detentions and unlawful interstate transfers involving Council of Europe member states. The report identifies 14 Council of Europe countries which appeared to have actively colluded in the CIA rendition programmes.

The Venice Commission was asked to prepare an opinion on the international legal obligations of Council of Europe member states in respect of secret detention facilities and interstate transport of prisoners.[433] In its conclusion, the Venice Commission stressed the responsibility of the Council of Europe's member states to secure that all persons within their jurisdiction enjoy internationally agreed fundamental rights (including the right to security of the person, freedom from torture and right to life).

If a Council of Europe state has reason to believe that an aeroplane crossing its airspace is carrying prisoners with the intention of transferring them to countries where they would face ill-treatment in violation of Article 3, it must take all necessary measures to prevent this and refuse the transit of persons where such a risk exists.

If a Council of Europe member state is informed or has a reasonable suspicion that any persons are being held incommunicado on foreign military bases on its territory, its responsibility under the ECHR is engaged unless it takes all measures within its power to bring this irregular situation to an end.

The Venice Commission also confirmed that the obligations arising out of the numerous bilateral and multilateral treaties in different fields such as collective self-defence, international civil aviation and military bases "do not prevent States from complying with their human rights obligations".

Findings of the Venice Commission

The responsibility of Council of Europe member states may be engaged under the Convention in the following situations arising from arrest and secret detention:

(a) failure to prevent arrest when in receipt of information prior to arrest by foreign agents within their jurisdiction;

(b) active or passive co-operation in secret detentions or failure to safeguard against the risk of disappearance or investigate substantiated claims that a person has been taken into unacknowledged custody;[434]

---

433 Opinion No. 363/2005, CDL-AD(2006)009, Strasbourg, 17 March 2006. Available at: www.venice.coe.int/docs/2006/CDL-AD(2006)009-e.asp.

434 *Kurt v. Turkey*, Application No. 24276/94, judgment of 25 May 2001. The investigation must be efficient, effective and impartial – see *Caloc v. France*, Application No. 33951/96, judgment of 20 July 2000.

(c) where state agents act *ultra vires* in co-operating with foreign states without the knowledge of their government;[435]

(d) failure to bring to an end suspected situations of irregular or incommunicado detention on its territory;

(e) failure to comply with the duty to inform the CPT of detention facilities on its territory and afford the committee access.

The transfer of prisoners to foreign states may only be legally effected via deportation, extradition,[436] or transit and transfer of sentenced persons to serve their sentence elsewhere where legal guarantees exist. Extradition and deportation are prohibited where the person faces Article 3 treatment in the receiving state[437] and applies to situations where the transfer is made through a Council of Europe member state. Diplomatic assurances[438] must be unequivocal and legally binding[439] but should not be accepted where there is substantial evidence that torture is practised in the receiving state.

Member states must take "all the necessary measures" to prevent aeroplanes crossing their airspace where they have serious reasons to believe they are transferring prisoners to countries where they face torture. This includes landing and searching civil planes or obtaining the consent of the flight captain to do so in respect of state planes.[440] All treaty obligations dealing with overflight permissions should ensure respect for human rights.

---

435 The opinion states at paragraph 120 that member states are accountable for all exercises of public power and are required to exercise effective oversight and control over the actions of security and intelligence agencies – see *Klass and Others v. Germany*, Series A, No. 28, judgment of 6 September 1978, in connection with *Leander v. Sweden*, Application No. 9248/81, judgment of 26 March 1987.

436 See, for example, *Öcalan v. Turkey*, Application No. 46221/95, judgment (GC) of 12 May 2005.

437 See *Soering v. the United Kingdom*, Application No. 140328/88, judgment of 7 July 1989.

438 See *Mamatkulov and Askerov v. Turkey*, Applications Nos. 46827/99 and 46951/99, judgment (GC) of 4 February 2005.

439 Decision of the CAT Committee, *Ahmed Hussein Mustafa Kamil Agiza v. Sweden*, decision CAT/C/34/D/233/2003, 24 May 2005.

440 The opinion notes at paragraph 146 that member states are obliged to "secure the most elementary rights" in aircraft in their airspace or military bases for foreign forces "regardless of acquiescence or connivance". See *Ilaşcu and Others v. Moldova and Russia*, Application No. 48787/99, judgment of 8 July 2004, *Riera Blume and Others v. Spain*, Application No. 37680/97, judgment of 14 January 2000, *Gongadze v. Ukraine*, Application No. 34056/02, judgment of 8 November 2005.

On 27 June 2006, in a resolution[441] and recommendation,[442] the Parliamentary Assembly of the Council of Europe called for oversight of foreign intelligence agencies operating in Europe and has even gone so far as to demand "human rights clauses" in military base agreements with the US.

---

441 Resolution 1507 (2006).

442 Recommendation 1754 (2006).

Part Three – The subsidiary protection of the European Court of Human Rights

1. The right of individual petition

Article 1 of the Convention requires all States Parties to the Convention to "secure to everyone within their jurisdiction the rights and freedoms" contained in the ECHR. Article 13 requires the states to give effect to Convention rights by providing victims of violations with "an effective remedy before a national authority". States thus have an obligation to refrain from violating the rights of individuals and to provide remedies for all violations of Convention rights. Victims of violations of their protected rights should therefore seek remedies at the national level.

Unfortunately, national remedies will not always be effective. In those cases the subsidiary protection of the ECHR organs is there.

Article 34 states:

> "The Court may receive applications from any person, non-governmental organisation or group of individuals claiming to be the victim of a violation by one of the High Contracting Parties of the rights set forth in the Convention or the protocols thereto. The High Contracting Parties undertake not to hinder in any way the effective exercise of this right."

The European Court is not a court of appeal from national authorities' or courts' refusals to grant asylum. The Court made this clear in both *Cruz Varas*[443] and *Vilvarajah*.[444] But where the national courts have proved unable or unwilling to offer the necessary protection or remedies, the subsidiary protection of the European Court is available under Article 34 of the Convention.

A comprehensive coverage of the exercise of the right of individual petition is beyond the scope of this book and what follows highlights only briefly those aspects of the Court's subsidiary protection which are of particular interest to those who work with asylum issues.

---

443 *Cruz Varas and Others v. Sweden*, Application No. 15576/89, judgment of 20 March 1991.

444 *Vilvarajah and Others v. the United Kingdom*, Applications Nos. 13163/87, 13164/87 and 13165/87, judgment of 30 October 1991.

Complaints under Article 34 can be brought in relation to any alleged violation of a Convention right, but the system has most frequently been used – in the context of asylum – by those at risk of being returned to face treatment prohibited by Article 3. However, as the composition of the Council of Europe and the nature of refugee flows have changed, new issues are arising under the Convention in many states where immediate expulsion is not the only or most important issue.

Prolonged, and sometimes unlawful detention, destitution – without the right to benefits or the right to work of those refused asylum but not being removed – and the more generic problem of the lack of status or documentation are just a few of the pressing problems. Victims of rights violations must look first and foremost to the state concerned to remedy the violation. If that state has demonstrably failed to meet its Convention obligations under Article 1 to secure the rights then it is required under Article 13 to provide a sufficient remedy. If the state also fails to do that the individual can, at that point, have recourse to the Convention organs.

The substantive content of the Convention law has been set out in detail above. This section is only concerned with the admissibility criteria and with the procedures before the European Court of Human Rights.

2. Interim measures – Rule 39

Perhaps the most important mechanism is the Court's power to indicate interim measures under Rule 39 of the Rules of Procedure. This power is regularly invoked to prevent an imminent expulsion pending the Court's substantive consideration of the complaint that the return would violate Articles 2 or 3.

In very urgent cases where there is danger that an applicant's return may give rise to a violation of Articles 2 or 3, the Court may decide to apply interim measures. Rule 39 (previously Rule 36) provides:

> "The Chamber, or where appropriate its President, may at the request of a party or of any other person concerned, or of its own motion, indicate to the parties any interim measure which it considers should be adopted in the interest of the parties or the proper conduct of the proceedings before it."

A threefold test must be satisfied in order for the Court to grant an interim measure. First there must be a threat of irreparable harm of a very serious nature. Second, the harm must be imminent and irremediable, and third, prima facie, there must be an arguable case.

Rule 39 is not applied lightly by the Court. Legal representatives who wish to have recourse to it should not underestimate the diligent preparation that is required for a Rule 39 application to succeed.

However, interim measures have been sought and granted in many cases. *D. v. the United Kingdom*[445] (to prevent removal of applicant to St Kitts as he was in the final stages of Aids), in *Soering*[446] (to prevent his extradition to the US where he would face capital charges for murder), in *Hilal*[447] (to prevent expulsion to Tanzania), in *Kalantari v. Germany*[448] and *Amrollahi v. Denmark*[449] (to prevent applicants' expulsion to Iran), and in *Shamayev and Others v. Georgia and Russia*[450] (to prevent the extradition of 11 Chechens from Georgia to Russia). Lawyers acting for several Somalis refused asylum in the Netherlands succeeded in obtaining the application of Rule 39 to a whole group of their clients. The judgment in *Salah Sheekh* was the "pilot" judgment on the merits for that group of cases. However, the granting of a Rule 39 indication should not be understood as leading automatically to a substantive finding that the expulsion will breach, or breached, Article 3.[451]

While in the majority of cases, the governments concerned will co-operate and respect the Rule 39 indications, there have been cases where governments have not complied with the decision of the Court to apply Rule 39 and have failed to give effect to the interim measures granted in the applicant's favour.

In the case of *Cruz Varas v. Sweden*[452] a Chilean had been refused asylum in Sweden and was the subject of removal directions. The Commission indicated to the Swedish Government that he should not be removed pending consideration of the case, but Sweden did not comply with the indication. The Court subsequently had to vote to determine whether the government's failure to comply with the Commission's request had violated the duty not to hinder the effective exercise of the right of individual petition under Article 34 and therefore whether it constituted a breach of the Convention. The Court came to the conclusion, by just 10 votes to nine, that the rule could not create a binding obligation on Convention states.[453] It noted, however, that, in the event of a finding of a substantive violation of the Convention, a failure to comply with a Rule 36 (now 39) indication would be a matter for serious concern. In its judgment, the Court gave important guidance as to the role and scope of Rule 36 (now 39).

---

445 *D. v. the United Kingdom*, Application No. 30240/96, judgment of 2 May 1997

446 *Soering v. the United Kingdom*, Application No. 14038/88, judgment of 7 July 1989.

447 *Hilal v. the United Kingdom*, Application No. 45276/99, judgment of 6 March 2001.

448 *Kalantari v. Germany*, Application No. 51342/99, judgment of 11 October 2001.

449 *Amrollahi v. Denmark*, Application No. 56811/00, judgment of 11 July 2002.

450 *Shamayev and Others v. Georgia and Russia*, Application No. 36378/02, judgment of 12 April 2005.

451 See, for example, *Mamatkulov and Askarov v. Turkey*, 2005.

452 *Cruz Varas and Others v. Sweden*, Application No. 15576/89, judgment of 20 March 1991.

453 Ibid., paragraphs 94-103.

The Court noted that an indication under Rule 36 (now 39) would only be given:

> "where it appears that irreparable damage would result from the implementation of the measure complained of. This might be the case where expulsion or extradition is imminent and the applicant alleges that he is likely to be treated contrary to Article 2 (the right to life) or [Article] 3 of the Convention in the receiving state. Normally Rule 36 (now Rule 39) will only apply to cases involving allegations of this nature. Further there must exist a certain degree of probability that a person would be subjected to treatment in breach of these provisions if sent to the country concerned. Evidence must thus be presented to the Commission which reveals such a risk."

This same issue arose in the case of *Čonka v. Belgium*,[454] where the applicants and 74 other Roma Gypsy refugees who had been refused asylum were put on board a plane to Slovakia, notwithstanding the fact that the Court had applied Rule 39 to indicate to the Belgian Government that they should not be expelled pending the Court's consideration of the case.

This unsatisfactory situation has been resolved by the judgment of the Grand Chamber in *Mamatkulov and Abdurasulovic v. Turkey*[455] in 2005. There the Court found a violation of Article 34 arising from the Turkish Government's failure to comply with the Rule 39 request not to extradite the applicant Uzbek nationals to Uzbekistan where they were wanted for an alleged terrorist attack on the President, and where they may have faced the death penalty. Assurances that the applicants will come to no harm upon their return will not absolve contracting states from the duty to comply with any Rule 39 indications.

The Court stated:

> "Any State Party to the Convention to which interim measures have been indicated in order to avoid irreparable harm being caused to the victim of an alleged violation must comply with those measures and refrain from any act or omission that will undermine the authority and effectiveness of the final judgment."[456]

The Grand Chamber's judgment found that the refusal to comply with a Rule 39 indication constituted a hindrance to the effective exercise of the individual right of petition under Article 34.

The violation of Article 34 can be twofold. In *Mamatkulov* the failure to comply not only resulted in the applicants' removal to the state where they claimed to be at risk, but also impeded their ability to continue to instruct their lawyers in the conduct of their complaint before the European Court. The situation was the same in *Aoulmi v. France*,[457] which affirmed the approach taken in *Mamatkulov*.

---

454 *Čonka v. Belgium*, Application No. 51564/99, judgment of 5 February 2002.

455 *Mamatkulov and Askarov v. Turkey*, Applications Nos. 46827/99 and 46951/99, judgment of 4 February 2005.

456 *Mamatkulov and Abdurasulovic v. Turkey*, Applications Nos. 46827/99 and 46951/99, judgment of 6 February, paragraph 110.

457 *Aoulmi v. France*, Application No. 50278/99, judgment of 17 January 2006.

In *Olaechea Cahuas v. Spain*,[458] the Court found the failure to comply with a Rule 39 indication was a violation of Article 34 even when the expulsion of the applicant did not prevent him from keeping in contact with his lawyers to pursue his application before the Court.

In none of the above cases did the Court (or at least its majority) find a substantive violation of Article 3. The free-standing nature of the requirement under Article 34 to comply with Rule 39 indications is thus affirmed.

3. Expediting cases

In cases where the stringent criteria for the application of interim measures under Rule 39 are not met, applicants can ask the Court to apply Rule 40 (urgent notification of an application to the respondent government) or Rule 41 (prioritising cases), both of which provide an additional mechanism for the speedy resolution of the case.

Time can be of the essence. Complaints brought to the European Court can typically take more than five years to reach judgment. Applying the urgent criteria, in *Soering v. the United Kingdom*, the time from lodging the application to judgment was a mere twelve months, and in *D. v. the United Kingdom*, the case was concluded within fifteen months.

4. Conditions to be fulfilled

The admissibility criteria are set out in Articles 34 and 35 of the Convention.

Victim status (Article 34) and representation

Applications can be received not only from those who have already become victims of violations, but also from those who are at risk of violations (such as expulsions) which have not yet occurred, or indirect victims (such as the family members of the principal victim).

Non-governmental organisations can only bring applications to the ECtHR in their own right if it is the organisation itself which is the victim of the violation. They cannot bring a complaint which is an *actio popularis*, that is where they are seeking to complain, in the abstract, about a law or practice which violates the human rights of people who are of concern to them.

NGOs can, however, act as the representatives of an individual applicant or a group of applicants (Rule 36(1)). Applicants can also bring complaints unrepresented, but would be ill-advised to do so unless they have no possibility of

---

458 *Olaechea Cahuas v. Spain*, Application No. 24668/03, judgment of 10 August 2006.

obtaining advice and representation from a lawyer or NGO familiar with the Convention's case law and its procedural mechanisms. However, under Rule 36 of the Court's Rules of Procedure, once the case has been "communicated" to the respondent government, applicants must be represented either by a lawyer authorised to practise in any Council of Europe member state (not necessarily the one against whom the complaint is brought). Anyone else who wishes to represent an applicant must, exceptionally, apply for and obtain the specific approval of the Court.

A victim of an expulsion order, or an individual with uncertain status, will lose victim status if the order is revoked or a residence permit is granted.[459]

Those persons whose applications for refugee status have been refused by a member state cannot be considered "victims" for the purpose of Article 34 unless they have come to the "end of a process which had nothing automatic about it" – in other words, unless they had received a final decision from a final court or tribunal which is immediately enforceable and not appealable.[460]

Conditions of admissibility (Article 35)

Exhaustion of domestic remedies

Applicants must exhaust all avenues of domestic remedy before they can lodge an application with the Court.[461]

Six-month rule

Applicants must lodge their application within six months from the date of the final domestic decision.[462] This rule is very strictly applied, but might theoretically be waived if the applicant was held in completely incommunicado detention at the relevant time, but neither ill-health nor ignorance of the rule have been accepted as justifying the failure to comply.

Under Article 35, paragraph 2(a), the application cannot be anonymous, but applicants who fear for themselves or their families can ask for their names to be withheld from the public.

The application must not be substantially the same as a matter which has already been examined by the Court or has already been submitted to another procedure of international investigation or settlement and contains no relevant new

---

459 See, for example, *Sisojeva and Others v. Latvia*, Application No. 60654/00, judgment (GC) of 15 January 2007.

460 *Vijayanathan and Pusparajah v. France*, Applications Nos. 17550/90 and 17825/90, judgment of 27 August 1992.

461 *Mogos and Krifka v. Germany*, Application No. 78084/01, decision of 27 March 2003.

462 *Alzery v. Sweden*, Application No. 10786/04, decision of 26 October 2004.

information. Representatives who are seeking to bring their client's situation to the attention of as many human rights bodies as possible in order to minimise the risk to the client of being expelled and maximise the publicity given to the case should be particularly wary of this provision.

Applicants must ensure that they complain about a matter which is regulated by the Convention. The Court has frequently pointed out that it has no jurisdiction to determine whether recognition as a refugee under the Geneva Convention has been rightly granted or withheld or discontinued (see, for example, *Ahmed v. Austria*). It can only decide whether an expulsion will violate Article 3 or another Convention article.

Protocol No. 14 (not yet in force at the time of writing) has added a new admissibility criterion to those previously contained in Article 35 of the ECHR.[463] The Court may declare an application inadmissible if it considers that the applicant has not suffered a significant disadvantage. This new criterion is unlikely to have any adverse effect on applications related to expulsion to face prohibited treatment. In expulsion cases the applicants will always be alleging a significant disadvantage such as threat to their lives and/or inhuman or degrading treatment and it is hard to see how any complaint that was not "manifestly ill-founded" under the present criteria would be excluded by the amended Article 35. It remains to be seen whether cases involving a minor technical breach of the provisions on, for example freedom of movement, might be susceptible to rejection under this new provision.

Many applications involving claims that expulsion would expose the applicants to significant harm are found to be inadmissible.

It is often a matter of determining whether the applicant's version of events is credible. Inconsistencies in the description of certain events, factual inaccuracies, and conflicting versions of events between their application to the Court and their statements to national authorities, combined with a lack of supporting documentary evidence, often stand in the way of such applicants and prevent them from crossing the admissibility hurdle. The sections on the jurisprudence of both the ECHR and of the UNCAT (above) are instructive. The failure to exhaust domestic remedies is also a frequent reason for cases being declared inadmissible – see, for example, *Bahaddar v. the Netherlands* – but the only remedies which have to be exhausted are those which are effective. In expulsion cases this means the remedy must have suspensive effect (see the section on Article 13 above).

The preceding sections of this little guide are designed to assist NGOs and the legal representatives of people in need of international protection, as well as decision makers within government, to a better understanding of the protection

---

463 Article 12 of Protocol No. 14 to the ECHR amending the control system of the Convention, CETS No. 194 and Explanatory Report. As of 14 December 2006, only one state party has not ratified the new protocol.

that the ECHR is able to offer, and thus enable them to approach both substantive issues and the subsidiary protection mechanisms with a better understanding of their roles.

If the Court finds that a violation of the Convention has occured, or would occur, the case passes to the Committee of Ministers, whose role is to oversee the execution of the judgment. This will involve the government paying any compensation or legal costs awarded by the Court, but also doing whatever may be necessary to put right the wrong which has occurred to the individual applicant. Where a systemic defect has been identified, the government may also be required to adopt general measures to ensure that such violations to not occur in the future.

5. Execution of judgments – The Committee of Ministers

The Committee of Ministers is responsible for supervising the execution of judgments of the Court. It meets six times a year for this express purpose. Article 46, paragraph 2, of the ECHR states: "The final judgment shall be transmitted to the Committee of Ministers, which shall supervise its execution."[464]

The Committee of Ministers therefore has the power to ensure that any just satisfaction awarded by the Court has been paid and that any individual measures for the benefit of the applicant have been met. Examples of such individual measures include the reopening of domestic proceedings,[465] and, in the case of *D. v. the United Kingdom*, the revocation of a decision to expel.[466] More recently, at its meeting on 6-7 June 2006, the Committee of Ministers considered individual measures to remedy immigrants' or asylum seekers' situations following the unlawful deportation or subjection to expulsion from Bulgaria *(Al-Nashif)*, Finland *(N.)*, Germany *(Keles)*, Netherlands *(Tuquabo-Tekle)* and Sweden *(Bader)*.

The Committee of Ministers will also supervise any general measures intended to prevent further similar violations. This is an effective way to combat systemic, repeat violations of the Convention by the contracting parties. Such measures may entail legislative, administrative or policy changes. Specific examples include instructions to relevant domestic authorities and education and/or training of public officials.

In order for the Committee to make a practical assessment of whether or not the states' obligations under the judgment have been fulfilled, the respondent state is required to provide information on the measures taken to ensure the execution of the case and could be invited formally to present an "action plan".

---

464 The Committee of Ministers' examination of cases can be researched at www.coe. int/t/CM and at www.coe.int/T/E/Human_Rights/execution.

465 *Jersild v. Denmark*, ComResDH(95)212, 11 September 1995.

466 *D. v. the United Kingdom*, ComResDH(98)10, 18 February 1998.

Applicants can submit in writing to the Committee their comments concerning the payment of just satisfaction or relating to any negative consequences of the violation that they might be suffering. In addition, the Committee of Ministers can also take into account any other source of information, if relevant.

However, non-enforcement of judgments remains a problem, and without strict supervision and the ability to impose sanctions, state inaction would effectively create a mockery of the European human rights judicial machinery. In October 2006, the Parliamentary Assembly of the Council of Europe (PACE), in Resolution 1516 (2006), stated that major structural deficiencies in judicial systems in Italy, Russia and Ukraine causing repeated violations of the European Convention on Human Rights represented a "serious danger to the rule of law".[467]

While the resolution did praise measures adopted in some states,[468] it still expressed grave concern in many areas. In particular, and in relation to domestic asylum processing procedures, the resolution highlighted that in Greece, no comprehensive plan has been presented to resolve the systemic problem of overcrowding of detention facilities (*Dougoz v. Greece*[469] and *Peers v. Greece*[470] judgments; Committee of Ministers Interim Resolution DH(2005)2), which has just been highlighted in yet another judgment (*Kaja v. Greece*).[471]

PACE Recommendation 1764 (2006) talks in terms of "increasing pressure and taking firmer measures" in cases of continuous non-compliance with a judgment by a member state due to either refusal, negligence or incapacity to take appropriate measures. The PACE urged the Committee of Ministers to reserve "special treatment" for the most important problems in the implementation of judgments, as detailed in Resolution 1516 (2006). Just what this special treatment will be remains to be seen.

---

467 Resolution 1516 (2006) on implementation of judgments of the European Court of Human Rights. See paragraph 10.

468 In Italy the Azzolini law of 2006 has created a legislative basis for a special procedure for the supervision of the implementation of judgments by the government and parliament; in Ukraine the adoption of a law in 2006 provides for a co-ordinated approach, under the supervision of the government agent before the court, to ensure the proper implementation of the Court's judgments. In the United Kingdom, a new practice was introduced in March 2006 consisting of progress reports on the implementation of Court judgments presented by the Joint Human Rights Committee of the British Parliament. In the case of *Slivenko v. Latvia* (Application No. 48321/99, judgment of 9 October 2003) the applicants' rights of permanent residence in Latvia have recently been restored, in line with the Committee requests. Latvia thus erased the effects of the applicants' expulsion to Russia found by the Court to be in violation of the ECHR.

469 Application No. 40907/98, judgment of 6 March 2001.

470 Application No. 28524/95, judgment of 19 April 2001.

471 Application No. 32927/03, judgment of 27 July 2006.

The Committee of Ministers meets for two days, six times a year, to supervise the execution of judgments. The review of the execution of judgments is therefore a long, slow process, even when the government is co-operative, and it is often not until years after a judgment that a final resolution closing the case is adopted.

Protocol No. 14 includes a provision relating to the refusal by a contracting party to abide by a final judgment of the Court. Article 16 of the protocol (amending Article 46 of the Convention) would enable the Committee of Ministers, by a majority of two thirds, to refer the question to the Court as to whether that state has failed to fulfil its obligations under Article 46, paragraph 1, of the Convention. However, while this provision would allow the Court to scrutinise the execution of its judgment, it does not provide the Court with any power to lay down sanctions if it finds a failure by the state to abide by Article 46, paragraph 1, of the ECHR. That said, the adverse publicity would surely apply substantial political, public and media pressure on the state to fulfil its obligations.

Currently, the 47 states have already ratified the protocol. The only state not to have done so at time of writing is Russia.

6. Asylum and the European Union

ECHR approach to EU law

Reference has been made throughout this book to the provisions of EU law which regulate the disposal of asylum-related issues in the 27 of the 47 Council of Europe states which are also member states of the EU. Some member states have exercised the option not to participate in or be bound by these measures.

Background

Member states began co-operation in the field of asylum outside the formal structures of the Community. The Schengen and Dublin Conventions were among the results of this early intergovernmental co-operation. Later, the Treaty on European Union formally recognised immigration and asylum as "matters of common interest of the European Union Member States in the Third Pillar".

Since the early 1990s the flow of persons seeking international protection in the European Union has been such that the member states decided to find common solutions to the challenge. In a Europe without internal borders it made sense to aim for an approximation of conditions for asylum seekers, so that one country would not seem more attractive a destination than another. The entry into force of the Treaty of Amsterdam in May 1999 marked a new stage in European Union asylum policy. Title IV of the Treaty provides for "an area of freedom, security and justice" and provides the legal basis for the

European Union to develop new powers to develop legislation on immigration and asylum matters. Since the major principles and aims were agreed at Tampere in 1999, numerous legal instruments on asylum have been produced.

The adoption of the Hague Programme in November 2004 set up the second phase instruments of the Common European Asylum system with a view to completion by 2010.

The European Union's Charter of Fundamental Rights includes in Article 18 the right to asylum.

EU law now regulates many aspects of asylum in more than half the states which are party to the ECHR. The various measures adopted at EU level and referred to here are directly applicable in all member states (except those who have opted out).

Four main EU legal instruments on asylum are of particular relevance to the ECHR and are already, or shortly will become, binding in all participating member states (a full list of the EU measures can be found in Appendix II).

1. Dublin II Regulation (Council Regulation 343/2003)

Establishes the criteria and mechanisms for determining the member state responsible for examining an asylum application lodged in one of the member states by a third country national. It is the successor of the Dublin Convention.

The Dublin Regulation replaced the earlier Dublin Convention, and did not originally apply to Denmark, but since 1 April 2006 an additional agreement is now in force extending its application (and that of the EURODAC Regulation) to Denmark.

2. Reception Conditions Directive (2003/9/EC)

Requires member states to provide basic support needs to asylum seekers whilst they are awaiting the determination of their claims. The directive requires states to provide a "dignified standard of living and comparable living conditions in all member states". It covers issues such as the right to information and documentation, provision of accommodation and financial support, access to employment and freedom of movement.

Ireland and Denmark have opted out of the directive.

3. Qualification Directive (2004/83/EC)

Provides legally binding criteria for the identification of Geneva Convention refugees and those entitled to "subsidiary protection". It also establishes a legal entitlement for those who fall within its ambit to significant substantive and procedural benefits. The Qualification Directive excludes from its ambit certain persons who are entitled to protection under international human rights law, although recital 6 of its preamble states "the main objective of this Directive is … to ensure that Member States apply common criteria for the identification of persons genuinely in need of international protection".

Denmark has opted out of the directive.

4. Asylum Procedures Directive (2005/85)

The Asylum Procedures Directive must be transposed by 1 December 2007.

It includes provisions on the first asylum country, safe third country and safe country of origin. Many have criticised the directive as a means to deny asylum seekers access to asylum procedures and to facilitate their transfer to countries outside the European Union. The United Nations High Commissioner for Refugees (UNHCR) has particularly criticised the directive in relation to the provisions on safe third country and non-suspensory appeals, neither of which appear to reflect the standards of the ECHR set out elsewhere in this book.

Denmark has opted out of the directive.

At the time of writing, as far as the author is aware, no cases are pending before the ECHR which complain about an act or omission of a Contracting Party to the ECHR resulting from the application of any of the EU asylum measures referred to in this book. The ECtHR may nevertheless be called upon in the future to consider two types of EU-related complaints in the context of asylum: first, where a state relies on the provisions of the relevant EU law to justify the violations of the ECHR which are alleged; and second where the acts or omissions in question are in themselves in violation of the provisions of the EU asylum regime and thus not in accordance with the law as required by many provisions of the Convention.

The Court has already examined the relationship between EU law and the ECHR on a number of occasions.

The case of *T.I. v. the United Kingdom* (considered above in the section on safe third countries) concerned an asylum seeker being returned from the United Kingdom to another member state under what was then the Dublin Convention. The Court considered whether, if there was a real risk that the individual concerned would be sent onward by the second state to the country where he or she claimed to be at risk of treatment contrary to Article 3 of the ECHR, the responsibility of the first state could be engaged. The Court found that it could, but did not engage in any detailed analysis of the inter-relationship between the two legal orders.

Matthews v. the United Kingdom[472] was a case brought under Article 3 of Protocol No. 1 of the ECHR concerning the inability of the citizens of Gibraltar to participate

---

472 Application No. 24833/94, judgment of 18 February 1999.

in elections to the European Parliament. The Court held that where the breach of a Convention right stemmed from the provisions of the primary EC treaties, member states would remain responsible for securing those rights. The responsibility of the United Kingdom was thus engaged under the Convention. The Court noted that measures adopted by the EC could not themselves be challenged before the Court as the EC was not itself a Contracting Party to the Convention.[473]

In *Bosphorus Airways v. Ireland*[474] the Court had to consider whether Ireland could be held accountable under the ECHR for actions which the court of the EU, the European Court of Justice (ECJ), had found it was required to carry out in order to comply with EU law in a situation where the interference with the peaceful enjoyment of possessions might otherwise have constituted a violation of Article 1, Protocol No. 1 of the ECHR. The Grand Chamber held that in the situation in question the protection of Convention rights was "equivalent" under the Convention system and EU law. The state in question would therefore be presumed not to have departed from its Convention obligations when fulfilling its obligations under EU law. This presumption would be rebutted if the protection was manifestly deficient. As such, the *ordre public* mission of the Convention would be found to outweigh international, EU interests. This is a compromise position between the protection of Convention rights and the freedom of member states to transfer sovereignty to international organisations such as the EU.

The Court has also recently considered a case where the violation of the Convention derived from the state's failure to implement EU law. In *Aristimuño Mendizabal v. France*,[475] the Court interpreted Article 8 of the Convention in line with Community law and in particular with member states' obligations to issue residence permits to citizens of other member states. The failure of the French to grant the applicant a residence permit for over fourteen years amounted to a breach of her Community law rights. The interference with her Article 8 rights was therefore not "in accordance with the law" as required by Article 8, paragraph 2 – irrespective of whether it was domestic law or Community law.

Analogous substantive and procedural rights exist in EU law under the Dublin II Regulation and the three directives mentioned above. Decisions, acts or omissions which are not in accordance with those measures may *ipso facto* violate the Convention.

---

473 Protocol No. 14 to the Convention (not in force at time of writing) foresees in Article 17 the possibility of the EU becoming a party to the ECHR in the future.

474 Application No. 45036/98, judgment of 30 June 2005.

475 Application No. 51431/99, judgment of 17 January 2006.

Conclusion

In many European countries a right of individual petition to an international tribunal exists only under the European Convention on Human Rights. The protection which the Convention organs offer to asylum seekers and refugees is consequently the most important safeguard against the interests of the state eclipsing the human rights of individuals. The last decade of the millennium saw important developments in the Convention jurisprudence in this field and the robust statements of principle made by the Court have made an important contribution to safeguarding the rights of those who are at risk from prohibited treatment in their country of origin. How the Court will continue to respond in the new millennium to the needs of those at risk not only in their countries of origin but exposed to racism and xenophobia in the host countries remains to be seen.

Appendix I – Selected Council of Europe instruments relating to asylum

Resolution 28 (1953) on the promotion of a European policy for assisting refugees, Parliamentary Assembly

European Agreement on the Abolition of Visas for Refugees, 1959

Recommendation 434 (1965) on the granting of the right of asylum to European refugees, Parliamentary Assembly

Protocol to the European Convention on Consular Functions concerning the Protection of Refugees, 1967

Resolution 14 (1967) on asylum to persons in danger of persecution, Committee of Ministers

Recommendation 564 (1969) on the acquisition by refugees of the nationality of their country of residence, Parliamentary Assembly

Recommendation 773 (1976) on *de facto* refugees, Parliamentary Assembly

Recommendation 775 (1976) on the preparation of an agreement concerning the transfer of responsibility for refugees who move lawfully from one member state of the Council of Europe to another, Parliamentary Assembly

Recommendation 787 (1976) on harmonisation of eligibility practice, Parliamentary Assembly

Recommendation 817 (1977) on the right of asylum, Parliamentary Assembly

Declaration on Territorial Asylum, 1977, Committee of Ministers

European Agreement on Transfer of Responsibility for Refugees, 1980

Recommendation No. R (81) 16 on the harmonisation of national procedures relating to asylum, 1981, Committee of Ministers

Recommendation No. R (84) 1 on the protection of persons not formally recognised as refugees, 1984, Committee of Ministers

Recommendation No. R (84) 21 on the acquisition by refugees of the nationality of the host country, 1984, Committee of Ministers

Recommendation 984 (1984) on the acquisition by refugees of the nationality of the receiving country, Parliamentary Assembly

Recommendation 1016 (1985) on living and working conditions of refugees and asylum seekers, Parliamentary Assembly

Recommendation 1088 (1988) on the right to territorial asylum, Parliamentary Assembly

Order No. 442 (1988) on the right to asylum, Parliamentary Assembly

Recommendation 1081 (1988) on the problems of nationality in mixed marriages, Parliamentary Assembly

Recommendation 1149 (1991) on Europe of 1992 and refugee policies, Parliamentary Assembly

Recommendation 1163 (1991) on the arrival of asylum seekers at European airports, Parliamentary Assembly

Recommendation 1144 (1991) on the situation of frontier populations and workers, Parliamentary Assembly

Recommendation 1211 (1993) on clandestine migration: traffickers and employers of clandestine migrants, Parliamentary Assembly

Recommendation 1236 (1994) on the right of asylum, Parliamentary Assembly

Recommendation 1237 (1994) on the situation of asylum seekers whose asylum applications have been rejected, Parliamentary Assembly

Recommendation No. R (94) 5 on guidelines to inspire practices of the member states of the Council of Europe concerning the arrival of asylum seekers at European airports, 1994, Committee of Ministers

Recommendation 1261 (1995) on the situation of immigrant women in Europe, Parliamentary Assembly

Recommendation 1277 (1995) on migrants, ethnic minorities and media, Parliamentary Assembly

Recommendation 1309 (1996) on the training of officials receiving asylum seekers at border points, Parliamentary Assembly

Recommendation 1327 (1997) on the protection and reinforcement of the human rights of refugees and asylum seekers in Europe, Parliamentary Assembly

Recommendation No. R (98) 13 on the right to an effective remedy by rejected asylum seekers against decisions on expulsion in the context of Article 3 of the European Convention on Human Rights, 1998, Committee of Ministers

Recommendation No. R (98) 15 on the training of officials who first come into contact with asylum seekers, in particular at border points, 1998, Committee of Ministers

Recommendation No. R (99) 12 on the return of rejected asylum seekers, 1999, Committee of Ministers

Recommendation 1440 (2000) on restrictions on asylum in the member states of the Council of Europe and the European Union, Parliamentary Assembly

Recommendation 1470 (2000) on the situation of gays and lesbians and their partners in respect of asylum and immigration in the member states of the Council of Europe, Parliamentary Assembly

Recommendation 1475 (2000) on the arrival of asylum seekers at European airports, Parliamentary Assembly

Resolution 1247 (2001) on female genital mutilation, Parliamentary Assembly

Recommendation 1525 (2001) on the United Nations High Commissioner for Refugees and the fiftieth anniversary of the Geneva Convention, Parliamentary Assembly

Recommendation 1544 (2001) on the *propiska* system applied to migrants, asylum seekers and refugees in Council of Europe member states: effects and remedies, Parliamentary Assembly

Recommendation 1547 (2002) on expulsion procedures in conformity with human rights and enforced with respect for safety and dignity, Parliamentary Assembly

Recommendation 1552 (2002) on vocational training of young asylum seekers in host countries, Parliamentary Assembly

Recommendation 1569 (2002) on the situation of refugees and internally displaced persons in the Federal Republic of Yugoslavia

Recommendation Rec(2003)5 to member states on measures of detention of asylum seekers, 2003, Committee of Ministers

Resolution 1327 (2003) on so-called "honour crimes", Parliamentary Assembly

Recommendation 1612 (2003) on the situation of Palestinian refugees, Parliamentary Assembly

Recommendation 1633 (2003) on the forced returns of Roma from the former Federal Republic of Yugoslavia, including Kosovo, to Serbia and Montenegro from Council of Europe member states, Parliamentary Assembly

Recommendation 1645 (2004) on access to assistance and protection for asylum seekers at European seaports and coastal areas, Parliamentary Assembly

Recommendation 1667 (2004) on the situation of refugees and displaced persons in the Russian Federation and some other CIS countries, Parliamentary Assembly

Recommendation Rec(2005)6 to member states on exclusion from refugee status in the context of Article 1 F of the Convention relating to the Status of Refugees of 28 July 1951, 2005, Committee of Ministers

Convention on the Avoidance of Statelessness in relation to State Succession, 2006, Committee of Ministers

Recommendation Rec(2006)21 to member states on internally displaced persons, 2006, Committee of Ministers

Resolution 1483 (2006) on the policy of return for failed asylum seekers in the Netherlands, Parliamentary Assembly

Recommendation 1755 (2006) on the human rights of irregular migrants, Parliamentary Assembly

Guidelines on human rights and the fight against terrorism, adopted by the Committee of Ministers of the Council of Europe at the 804th meeting of the Ministers' Deputies

For the purposes of this book Guideline XII is most relevant.

"XII. Asylum, return *('refoulement')* and expulsion

1. All requests for asylum must be dealt with on an individual basis. An effective remedy must lie against the decision taken. However, when the State has serious grounds to believe that the person who seeks to be granted asylum has participated in terrorist activities, refugee status must be refused to that person.

2. It is the duty of a State that has received a request for asylum to ensure that the possible return *('refoulement')* of the applicant to his/her country of origin or to another country will not expose him/her to the death penalty, to torture or to inhuman or degrading treatment or punishment. The same applies to expulsion.

3. Collective expulsion of aliens is prohibited.

4. In all cases, the enforcement of the expulsion or return *('refoulement')* order must be carried out with respect for the physical integrity and for the dignity of the person concerned, avoiding any inhuman or degrading treatment."

The full text may be found at:
www.coe.int/T/E/Human_rights/h-inf(2002)8eng.pdf

Appendix II – Key European Union texts relating to asylum

Dublin Convention determining the State responsible for examining applications for asylum lodged in one of the Member States of the European Communities and measures for implementation (15 June 1990)

Resolution on manifestly unfounded applications for asylum (30 November 1992)

Resolution on a harmonised approach to questions concerning host third countries (30 November 1992)

Conclusions on countries in which there is generally no serious risk of persecution (30 November 1992)

Decision establishing a clearing house (CIREA) (30 November 1992)

Decision setting up a centre for Information Discussion and Exchange on the Crossing of Borders and Immigration (CIREFI) (30 November 1992)

Recommendation regarding practices followed by Member States on expulsion (30 November 1992)

Recommendation regarding transit for the purposes of expulsion (30 November 1992)

Resolution on certain common guidelines as regards the admission of particularly vulnerable persons from the former Yugoslavia

Resolution on minimum guarantees for asylum procedures (20 June 1995)

Joint Position on the harmonised application of the definition of the term "refugee" in Article 1 of the Geneva Convention relating to the Status of Refugees (4 March 1996)

Regulation 2725/2000 of 11 December 2000 concerning the establishment of "Eurodac" for the comparison of fingerprints for the effective application of the Dublin Convention

Regulation 539/2001 of 15 March 2001 listing the third countries whose nationals must be in possession of visas when crossing the external borders and those whose nationals are exempt from that requirement

Decision 258/2001 of 15 March 2001 concerning the conclusion of an Agreement between the European Community and the Republic of Iceland and the Kingdom of Norway concerning the criteria and mechanisms for establishing the state responsible for examining a request for asylum lodged in a Member State or Iceland or Norway

Directive 2001/40 of 28 May 2001 on the mutual recognition of decisions on the expulsion of third country nationals

Directive 2001/51 of 28 June 2001 supplementing the provisions of Article 26 of the Convention implementing the Schengen Agreement of 14 June 1985

Directive 2001/55 of 20 July 2001 on minimum standards for giving temporary protection in the event of a mass influx of displaced persons and on measures promoting a balance of efforts between Member States in receiving such persons and bearing the consequences thereof

Council Framework Decision of 13 June 2002 on the European Arrest Warrant and the surrender procedures between Member States

Council Framework Decision of 28 November 2002 on the strengthening of the penal framework to prevent the facilitation of unauthorised entry, transit and residence

Directive 2002/90 of 28 November 2002 defining the facilitation of unauthorised entry, transit and residence

Directive 2003/9 of 27 January 2003 laying down minimum standards for the reception of asylum seekers

Regulation 343/2003 of 18 February 2003 establishing the criteria and mechanisms for determining the Member State responsible for examining an asylum application lodged in one of the Member States by a third-country national

Regulation 1560/2003 of 2 September 2003 laying down detailed rules for the application of Council Regulation 343/2003 of 18 February 2003

Directive 2003/86 of 22 September 2003 on the right to family reunification filed by the European Parliament in the Court of Justice of the European Communities

Directive 2003/109 of 25 November 2003 on the status of third-country nationals who are long-term residents

Directive 2004/38 on the right of citizens of the Union and their family members to move and reside freely within the territory of the European Union

Directive 2004/83 of 29 April 2004 on minimum standards for the qualification and status of third country nationals or stateless persons as refugees or as persons who otherwise need international protection and the content of the protection granted

Directive 2005/85 of 1 December 2005 on minimum standards on procedures in member states for granting and withdrawing refugee status (to be transposed by EU Member States by 1 December 2007)

Appendix III – Dates of entry into force of the ECHR and its protocols by member states of the Council of Europe
(as at 26 June 2006)

Note that all member states of the Council of Europe are now party to the ECHR.

State	Convention ETS No. 5	Protocol No. 1 ETS No. 9	Protocol No. 4 ETS No. 46	Protocol No. 6 ETS No. 114	Protocol No. 7 ETS No. 117	Protocol No. 12 ETS No. 177	Protocol No. 13 ETS No. 187
Albania	02/10/96	02/10/96	02/10/96	01/10/00	01/01/97	01/04/05	
Andorra	22/01/96			01/02/96			01/07/03
Armenia	26/04/02	26/04/02	26/04/02	01/10/03	01/07/02	01/04/05	
Austria	03/09/58	03/09/58	18/09/69	01/03/85	01/11/88		01/05/04
Azerbaijan	15/04/02	15/04/02	15/04/02	01/05/02	01/07/02		
Belgium	14/06/55	14/06/55	21/09/70	01/01/99			01/10/03
Bosnia and Herzegovina	12/07/02	12/07/02	12/07/02	01/08/02	01/10/02	01/04/05	01/11/03
Bulgaria	07/09/92	07/09/92	04/11/00	01/10/99	01/02/01		01/07/03
Croatia	05/11/97	05/11/97	05/11/97	01/12/97	01/02/98	01/04/05	01/07/03
Cyprus	06/10/62	06/10/62	03/10/89	01/02/00	01/12/00	01/04/05	01/07/03
Czech Republic	01/01/93	01/01/93	01/01/93	01/01/93	01/01/93		01/11/04
Denmark	03/09/53	18/05/54	02/05/68	01/03/85	01/11/88		01/07/03
Estonia	16/04/96	16/04/96	16/04/96	01/05/98	01/07/96		01/06/04
Finland	10/05/90	10/05/90	10/05/90	01/06/90	01/08/90	01/04/05	01/03/05
France	03/05/74	03/05/74	03/05/74	01/03/86	01/11/88		
Georgia	20/05/99	07/06/02	13/04/00	01/05/00	01/07/00	01/04/05	01/09/03
Germany	03/09/53	13/02/57	01/06/68	01/08/89			01/02/05
Greece	28/11/74	28/11/74		01/10/98	01/11/88		01/06/05
Hungary	05/11/92	05/11/92	05/11/92	01/12/92	01/02/93		01/11/03
Iceland	03/09/53	18/05/54	02/05/68	01/06/87	01/11/88		01/03/05
Ireland	03/09/53	18/05/54	29/10/68	01/07/94	01/11/01		01/07/03
Italy	26/10/55	26/10/55	27/05/82	01/01/89	01/02/92		
Latvia	27/06/97	27/06/97	27/06/97	01/06/99	01/09/97		
Liechtenstein	08/09/82	14/11/95		01/12/90	01/05/05		01/07/03
Lithuania	20/06/95	24/05/96	20/06/95	01/08/99	01/09/95		01/05/04

State	Convention ETS No. 5	Protocol No. 1 ETS No. 9	Protocol No. 4 ETS No. 46	Protocol No. 6 ETS No. 114	Protocol No. 7 ETS No. 117	Protocol No. 12 ETS No. 177	Protocol No. 13 ETS No. 187
Luxembourg	03/09/53	18/05/54	02/05/68	01/03/85	01/07/89		
Malta	23/01/67	23/01/67	05/06/02	01/04/91	01/04/03		01/07/03
Moldova	12/09/97	12/09/97	12/09/97	01/10/97	01/12/97		
Monaco	30/11/05		30/11/05	01/12/05	01/02/05		01/03/06
Netherlands	31/08/54	31/08/54	23/06/82	01/05/86		01/04/05	
Norway	03/09/53	18/05/54	02/05/68	01/11/88	01/01/89		01/12/05
Poland	19/01/93	10/10/94	10/10/94	01/11/00	01/03/03		
Portugal	09/11/78	09/11/78	09/11/78	01/11/86			01/02/04
Romania	20/06/94	20/06/94	20/06/94	01/07/94	01/09/94		01/08/03
Russian Federation	05/05/98	05/05/98	05/05/98		01/08/98		
San Marino	22/03/89	22/03/89	22/03/89	01/04/89	01/06/89	01/04/05	01/08/03
Serbia	03/03/04	03/03/04	03/03/04	01/04/04	01/06/04	01/04/05	01/07/04
Slovakia	01/01/93	01/01/93	01/01/93	01/01/93	01/01/93		01/12/05
Slovenia	28/06/94	28/06/94	28/06/94	01/07/94	01/09/94		01/04/04
Spain	04/10/79	27/11/90		01/03/85			
Sweden	03/09/53	18/05/54	02/05/68	01/03/85	01/11/88		01/08/03
Switzerland	28/11/74			01/11/87	01/11/88		01/07/03
"The former Yugoslav Republic of Macedonia"	10/04/97	10/04/97	10/04/97	01/05/97	01/07/97		01/11/04
Turkey	18/05/54	18/05/54		01/12/03			
Ukraine	11/09/97	11/09/97	11/09/97	01/05/00	01/12/97		01/07/03
United Kingdom	03/09/53	18/05/54		01/06/99			01/02/04

Note that Montenegro became the 47th Member of the Council of Europe on 11 May 2007. The ECHR entered into force in Montenegro on 6 June 2006.

For up-to-date information see
www.echr.coe.int/ECHR/EN/Header/Basic+Texts/Basic+Texts/Dates+of+ratification+of+the+European+Convention+on+Human+Rights+and+Additional+Protocols/

Appendix IV – Countries which have accepted the right of individual petition under the United Nations Convention against Torture
(as at 30 November 2006)

Algeria
Argentina
Australia
Austria
Azerbaijan
Belgium
Bolivia
Bosnia and Herzegovina
Brazil
Bulgaria
Burundi
Cameroon
Canada
Chile
Costa Rica
Croatia
Cyprus
Czech Republic
Denmark
Ecuador
Finland

France
Georgia
Germany
Ghana
Greece
Guatemala
Hungary
Iceland
Ireland
Italy
Liechtenstein
Luxembourg
Malta
Mexico
Monaco
Montenegro
Morocco
Netherlands
New Zealand
Norway
Paraguay

Peru
Poland
Portugal
Russian Federation
Senegal
Serbia
Seychelles
Slovakia
Slovenia
South Africa
Spain
Sweden
Switzerland
Togo
Tunisia
Turkey
Ukraine
Uruguay
Venezuela

For up-to-date information see:
www.ohchr.org/english/bodies/cat/stat3.htm

Sales agents for publications of the Council of Europe
Agents de vente des publications du Conseil de l'Europe

BELGIUM/BELGIQUE
La Librairie Européenne -
The European Bookshop
Rue de l'Orme, 1
B-1040 BRUXELLES
Tel.: +32 (0)2 231 04 35
Fax: +32 (0)2 735 08 60
E-mail: order@libeurop.be
http://www.libeurop.be

Jean De Lannoy
Avenue du Roi 202 Koningslaan
B-1190 BRUXELLES
Tel.: +32 (0)2 538 43 08
Fax: +32 (0)2 538 08 41
E-mail: jean.de.lannoy@dl-servi.com
http://www.jean-de-lannoy.be

CANADA
Renouf Publishing Co. Ltd.
1-5369 Canotek Road
OTTAWA, Ontario K1J 9J3, Canada
Tel.: +1 613 745 2665
Fax: +1 613 745 7660
Toll-Free Tel.: (866) 767-6766
E-mail: order.dept@renoufbooks.com
http://www.renoufbooks.com

CZECH REPUBLIC/
RÉPUBLIQUE TCHÈQUE
Suweco CZ, s.r.o.
Klecakova 347
CZ-180 21 PRAHA 9
Tel.: +420 2 424 59 204
Fax: +420 2 848 21 646
E-mail: import@suweco.cz
http://www.suweco.cz

DENMARK/DANEMARK
GAD
Vimmelskaftet 32
DK-1161 KØBENHAVN K
Tel.: +45 77 66 60 00
Fax: +45 77 66 60 01
E-mail: gad@gad.dk
http://www.gad.dk

FINLAND/FINLANDE
Akateeminen Kirjakauppa
PO Box 128
Keskuskatu 1
FIN-00100 HELSINKI
Tel.: +358 (0)9 121 4430
Fax: +358 (0)9 121 4242
E-mail: akatilaus@akateeminen.com
http://www.akateeminen.com

FRANCE
La Documentation française
(diffusion/distribution France entière)
124, rue Henri Barbusse
F-93308 AUBERVILLIERS CEDEX
Tél.: +33 (0)1 40 15 70 00
Fax: +33 (0)1 40 15 68 00
E-mail: commande@ladocumentationfrancaise.fr
http://www.ladocumentationfrancaise.fr

Librairie Kléber
1 rue des Francs Bourgeois
F-67000 STRASBOURG
Tel.: +33 (0)3 88 15 78 88
Fax: +33 (0)3 88 15 78 80
E-mail: francois.wolfermann@librairie-kleber.fr
http://www.librairie-kleber.com

GERMANY/ALLEMAGNE
AUSTRIA/AUTRICHE
UNO Verlag GmbH
August-Bebel-Allee 6
D-53175 BONN
Tel.: +49 (0)228 94 90 20
Fax: +49 (0)228 94 90 222
E-mail: bestellung@uno-verlag.de
http://www.uno-verlag.de

GREECE/GRÈCE
Librairie Kauffmann s.a.
Stadiou 28
GR-105 64 ATHINAI
Tel.: +30 210 32 55 321
Fax.: +30 210 32 30 320
E-mail: ord@otenet.gr
http://www.kauffmann.gr

HUNGARY/HONGRIE
Euro Info Service kft.
1137 Bp. Szent István krt. 12.
H-1137 BUDAPEST
Tel.: +36 (06)1 329 2170
Fax: +36 (06)1 349 2053
E-mail: euroinfo@euroinfo.hu
http://www.euroinfo.hu

ITALY/ITALIE
Licosa SpA
Via Duca di Calabria, 1/1
I-50125 FIRENZE
Tel.: +39 0556 483215
Fax: +39 0556 41257
E-mail: licosa@licosa.com
http://www.licosa.com

MEXICO/MEXIQUE
Mundi-Prensa México, S.A. De C.V.
Río Pánuco, 141 Delegacíon Cuauhtémoc
06500 MÉXICO, D.F.
Tel.: +52 (01)55 55 33 56 58
Fax: +52 (01)55 55 14 67 99
E-mail: mundiprensa@mundiprensa.com.mx
http://www.mundiprensa.com.mx

NETHERLANDS/PAYS-BAS
De Lindeboom Internationale Publicaties b.v.
M.A. de Ruyterstraat 20 A
NL-7482 BZ HAAKSBERGEN
Tel.: +31 (0)53 5740004
Fax: +31 (0)53 5729296
E-mail: books@delindeboom.com
http://www.delindeboom.com

NORWAY/NORVÈGE
Akademika
Postboks 84 Blindern
N-0314 OSLO
Tel.: +47 2 218 8100
Fax: +47 2 218 8103
E-mail: support@akademika.no
http://www.akademika.no

POLAND/POLOGNE
Ars Polona JSC
25 Obroncow Street
PL-03-933 WARSZAWA
Tel.: +48 (0)22 509 86 00
Fax: +48 (0)22 509 86 10
E-mail: arspolona@arspolona.com.pl
http://www.arspolona.com.pl

PORTUGAL
Livraria Portugal
(Dias & Andrade, Lda.)
Rua do Carmo, 70
P-1200-094 LISBOA
Tel.: +351 21 347 42 82 / 85
Fax: +351 21 347 02 64
E-mail: info@livrariaportugal.pt
http://www.livrariaportugal.pt

RUSSIAN FEDERATION/
FÉDÉRATION DE RUSSIE
Ves Mir
9a, Kolpacnhyi per.
RU-101000 MOSCOW
Tel.: +7 (8)495 623 6839
Fax: +7 (8)495 625 4269
E-mail: orders@vesmirbooks.ru
http://www.vesmirbooks.ru

SPAIN/ESPAGNE
Mundi-Prensa Libros, s.a.
Castelló, 37
E-28001 MADRID
Tel.: +34 914 36 37 00
Fax: +34 915 75 39 98
E-mail: libreria@mundiprensa.es
http://www.mundiprensa.com

SWITZERLAND/SUISSE
Van Diermen Editions – ADECO
Chemin du Lacuez 41
CH-1807 BLONAY
Tel.: +41 (0)21 943 26 73
Fax: +41 (0)21 943 36 05
E-mail: info@adeco.org
http://www.adeco.org

UNITED KINGDOM/ROYAUME-UNI
The Stationery Office Ltd
PO Box 29
GB-NORWICH NR3 1GN
Tel.: +44 (0)870 600 5522
Fax: +44 (0)870 600 5533
E-mail: book.enquiries@tso.co.uk
http://www.tsoshop.co.uk

UNITED STATES and CANADA/
ÉTATS-UNIS et CANADA
Manhattan Publishing Company
468 Albany Post Road
CROTTON-ON-HUDSON, NY 10520, USA
Tel.: +1 914 271 5194
Fax: +1 914 271 5856
E-mail: Info@manhattanpublishing.com
http://www.manhattanpublishing.com

Council of Europe Publishing/Editions du Conseil de l'Europe
F-67075 Strasbourg Cedex
Tel.: +33 (0)3 88 41 25 81 – Fax: +33 (0)3 88 41 39 10 – E-mail: publishing@coe.int – Website: http://book.coe.int